States and
Urban-Based
REVOLUTIONS

States and
Urban-Based
REVOLUTIONS

IRAN AND NICARAGUA

F A R I D E H   F A R H I

UNIVERSITY OF ILLINOIS PRESS
Urbana and Chicago

© 1990 by the Board of Trustees of the University of Illinois
Manufactured in the United States of America
C 5 4 3 2 1

This book is printed on acid-free paper.

Library of Congress Cataloging-in-Publication Data

Farhi, Farideh.
    States and urban-based revolutions: Iran and Nicaragua / Farhi
Farideh.
        p. cm.
    ISBN 0-252-01710-2 (alk. paper)
    1. Iran—Politics and government—1979–   2. Nicaragua—Politics
and government—1979–   3. Revolutions—Case studies. I. Title.
DS318.825.F35 1990
955.05'4—dc20   89-48175
                                                           CIP

For my parents

Contents

Acknowledgments

The origins of this book go back to my dissertation on the Iranian revolution. Hence, it should be of no surprise that my biggest intellectual debt is to Edward S. Greenberg, my advisor. His solid advice and timely encouragement transformed vague ideas into concrete sentences. I am thankful to him not only for the time and energy he devoted to guiding this project in its dissertation stage but also for his friendship. Ed was truly an ideal advisor. Other members of my dissertation committee, Sam Fitch, Ted Gurr, and Tom Mayer, made valuable suggestions that forced me to sharpen my argument. Classes taken from Dennis Eckart, Horst Mewes, and Bob Stover also influenced me intellectually. More important, these three touched me personally. Horst was always kind, Dennis always offered me a shoulder to cry on, and Bob was simply himself—one of the nicest people I have ever met. Many friends (Ginny Bollinger, Homeyra Dine Pajouh, Steve Kelly, Linde Rachel, Ahmad Sarshar, Thad Tecza, Jean Umbreit, Karen Wiley, and Jeannie Yamine) contributed to the production of the dissertation by sharing ideas and helping me adapt to graduate life. I thank them all.

In the process of transforming the dissertation into a comparative analysis of urban-based revolutions, I relied heavily on the advice of others. Strangely, I do not know the two people who have had the most impact on the structure and content of this book. Their anonymous reviews exemplified critical commentary at its best. I am still hopeful that the ethos of "professionalism" can be overcome one of these days and I can thank them in person. Kathy Ferguson, Wally Goldfrank, Ben Kerkvliet, Quee-Young Kim, Peter Manicas, Bob Stauffer, and Majid Tehranian were kind enough to read different versions or parts of the manuscript carefully and comment on them. I did not do everything they asked me to do, but I did find all their suggestions very valuable. Larry Malley (now of Duke University Press) and Richard Wentworth of the University of Illinois Press worked very hard to find the right readers for my manuscript, and Jane Mohraz's expert copy editing was a very important part of this book's becoming a reality. Some of the material in chapters 1 and 4 has appeared in journal articles. I am grateful to the editors of *Comparative Political Studies* and the *Journal of Developing Societies* for allowing me to use parts of those articles.

Having two children while trying to fulfill the obligations of teaching and writing has been rather difficult. To be sure, I had incredible cooperation from Semira and Kaveh. They both let me work until the day I was giving birth and sent me back to work in no time. But I found that even cooperative kids come into conflict with the requirements of a university position. Fortunately, I have had a very strong support network. Effat and Ahmad Farhi (to whom this book is dedicated) and Afsar Rezaee Nikou literally came from the other side of the planet to bring some order into my life and help with the children, while Janeen Ancheta went out of her way to be kind to my daughter. Members of my extended family were always ready to give support, even through very expensive overseas phone calls. Soraya Abachi, Lindy Aquino, Beth Byerly, Connie Fisher, Andy Hoffman, Huma Ibrahim, Kathie Kane, Masahide Kato, Chelsea Kent, Cindy Kobayashi, Gerry Kosasa-Terry, Maivan Clech Lam, Elizabeth Lee, Vivian Luning, Neal Milner, Carole Moon, Nipa Rahim, Marta Savigliano, Carolyn Stephenson, Phyllis Turnbull, and Julie Wuthnow did many, many favors, discussed ideas with me, and listened to my complaints about the gender-based injustices of academic life.

Finally, I must say that this book would not have been completed without Ardalan R. Nikou's hard work, untiring friendship, and boundless patience. Ardalan did not merely support my endeavors; he made them possible. My gratitude is matched only by my feelings for him.

Introduction

The idea of comparing the Nicaraguan and Iranian revolutions was an uneasy one in the beginning. After all, on the surface, they only had one thing in common: the year revolutionaries brought down their respective repressive and isolated governments. What else could a relatively large oil-producing nation have in common with a very small agroexporting country? But I could not let go of the idea. After all, it was the comparison of not Iran and Nicaragua but revolutions in these two countries that was of concern. It was the event, which happens so rarely, that motivated me to ask questions. I kept searching for the answers to the "big" questions asked about revolutions. Given the obvious differences between the two, were there similar dynamics that could explain both revolutions? How can we account for the loss of so many lives in Nicaragua as opposed to the relatively nonviolent process in Iran? I also had other questions. For instance, why did the Sandinistas quickly declare an end to the death penalty, whereas public executions became a part of revolutionary celebration in Iran? Is ideology a sufficient explanation? Similarly, is ideology an adequate explanation of the manifest differences in outcomes? The questions went on. To be sure, I was not fully comfortable with these questions. By merely posing them, I told myself, I could be forcing an artificial explanation on these two very different countries, which happened to experience something called revolution.

This book is the result of my struggle to answer questions about these two revolutions (and perhaps other similar revolutions as well) and yet to be conscious of the particularity of the events I am trying to explain. Despite misgivings, I continue to be committed to a comparative historical approach.[1] The essence of this approach is to compare in detail a small number of cases within an explicit theoretical framework. As such, this strategy is not intended to be a mechanism for building theory.

In fact, this kind of comparison presupposes theory. This theory defines the subject, provides the criteria for the selection of appropriate cases, and supplies concepts and hypotheses.[2] In other words, theory is not inductively derived from the analysis itself but is deduced from "macro-sociological imagination," informed by contemporary theoretical debates and historical evidence. The usefulness of comparative history is its ability to act as an important check on theoretical explanation. By encouraging us to make explicit the causal arguments suggested by grand theoretical perspectives, this approach leads us closer to the ultimate objective, which is the illumination of causal regularities across sets of historical cases.[3]

It is important to understand the limitations of this objective. Generalization from particular cases is not what is at stake. The essence of comparative history is to maintain the particularity of each case while accepting that each particularity is shaped by general forces operating at the societal or global level. Accordingly, the intention is to expose these forces as they impinge on quite specific and unique circumstances in the hope of shedding light on historical specificities as well as the changing structures in the larger world-historical context that make contemporary revolutions not utterly unlike "classic" revolutions but also not totally similar to them. The reader will determine whether or not the way I have dealt with the events does justice to the complex history of these two countries. I am not a country specialist and my inability to read Spanish has clearly prevented me from having full access to the rich primary and secondary material on Nicaragua. I have also not used many materials written in Persian, although I did read many of them. In general, I think the material originally published in (or translated into) English on both countries is vast enough in depth and scope to have allowed me to find basic information without difficulty. I have seen my task as one of interpreting this rich scholarship. My hope is that even country special-ists will find the way I think about these revolutions useful, despite simplification here and there.

Let me just make a short plea for my approach by saying that two important similarities—the type of states that came under attack and the urban nature of mobilization—gave me the incentive to insist on a comparative study. These similarities, in turn, generated the following questions as the basis of this study:

1. What are the sociostructural and world-historical underpin-nings of the economic system that create the *potential* for diverse urban oppositional groupings to coalesce?

2. Since the economic and social factors arising from uneven development of capitalism are present in most Third World countries,

what are the structural factors that allow such a coalescence to become actualized?

    a. Is the nature of regimes—modernizing, narrow, military-based dictatorships—important in creating such a broad opposition?

    b. Can sociostructural, historical, and cultural factors help explain the massive mobilization itself? In particular, is there anything in the structure of the urban community itself that makes collective action possible?

    3. Since the actual mobilization of the population does not ensure the fall of any regime, is there anything in the structure of states that can help explain why some types of states are less effective in responding to popular uprising? Are some states in the Third World structurally too weak to deal with the internal and international pressures imposed on them?

    4. Finally, how does urban mobilization affect revolutionary outcome?

    As mentioned, these questions are clearly not generated in a theoretical void. As I will discuss in chapter 1, scholarship on revolution has been going through intense debates on the role of the state, ideology, collective action, and the international environment. This book will tackle the issues raised by these debates in the hope of contributing to them. I will argue that recent revolutions in Iran and Nicaragua force us to rethink some of the arguments made in relation to: (1) the kinds of pressure that are imposed on states in the periphery of the global economy and the types of states that are more prone to breakdown in the face of these pressures, (2) the effects of urban mobilization on revolutionary processes and outcome, and (3) the role of ideology in creating the revolutionary situation and producing the outcome. Accordingly, chapters 2, 3, and 4 will be successively devoted to understanding the role of the state, urban mobilization, and ideology in the unfolding of the Iranian and Nicaraguan revolutions. By laying out my argument in this way, I can draw from it to explain in chapter 5 important similarities and differences in outcomes.

NOTES

    1. Obviously, there is no agreement on exactly what is a comparative historical approach and what it is good for. Here, I am introducing my particular understanding of it. For a succinct discussion of the various ways comparative history is used, see T. Skocpol and M. Somers, "The Uses of Comparative History

in Macrosocial Inquiry," *Comparative Studies of Society and History* 22 (July 1980), pp. 174–97.

2. What this means is that the cases are chosen for theoretical relevance and not statistical representation.

3. T. Skocpol, *States and Social Revolutions: A Comparative Analysis of France, Russia and China* (Cambridge: Cambridge University Press, 1979), pp. 33–40.

1

Revolutions in Peripheral Formations:
Questions and Concepts

In the social sciences, there has been a recent revival of interest in, and a new orientation to, the subject of revolution.[1] This new orientation has generally called for the historical grounding of theories of revolutions[2] and has been keen on developing more refined categories—e.g., social revolution, revolution from above, agrarian revolution—as opposed to lumping revolutions under more generalized categories, such as internal war or political violence. More important, the new orientation has called for sharper focus on the structural details and goals of different states and the relationships of these states to dominant classes, the intrusion of international factors, and the structure of peasant communities.

While important contributions have been made by others, Theda Skocpol's *States and Social Revolutions* has generated the most interest. It is perhaps the most comprehensive attempt to bring together the new concerns about the role of the state, the structure of peasant communities, and the role of international factors in understanding the processes and outcomes of revolutions. Her rigorous method of comparative historical analysis and the appeal of her hypotheses create an imperative to broaden the empirical bases of her investigations. In this study, I do this by focusing on the Iranian and Nicaraguan cases.

The Iranian and Nicaraguan revolutions are particularly interesting since, at least on the surface, they seem to vary significantly from the general revolutionary pattern unraveled by Skocpol, as well as other recent theories of revolution.[3] At least three aspects of these revolutions appear to pose problems for Skocpol's formulation.[4] First, in *States and*

Social Revolutions, Skocpol insists that the "launching" of revolutions must be found in the crisis centered in the structures and situations of the prerevolutionary state. Presumably, the state must crumble. This is particularly troublesome, given the apparent strength of the Iranian armed forces and the Nicaraguan National Guard as well as the absence of both fiscal crisis (unlike France in 1789) and international pressure (unlike Russia in 1917), thought to be necessary for the collapse of authoritarian regimes.

Second, in contrast to most twentieth-century revolutions, both of these revolutions had an overwhelming urban character, partly because Iran and Nicaragua had higher levels of urbanization than did other countries experiencing social revolutions (with the exception of Cuba).[5] While it is true that many of the participants were of rural origin, these revolutions were nonetheless urban events, produced by the condition of their major cities in the 1970s. Even in Nicaragua, where cities and the government experienced guerrilla assaults from the countryside, mobilization of peasant armies was insignificant compared with that in Asia.[6] Furthermore, as in the Iranian case, support from the urban intermediate classes and other urban elements played a crucial part in the triumph of the revolution. In both cases, diverse oppositional groupings enjoyed the active support of the clergy and, unlike in El Salvador, significant sectors of the business community. More important, the urban character affected the means by which the two regimes were confronted by their opponents— political as opposed to armed conflict, until the last stages. The general strike, which lasted nearly six months in Iran, was one of the longest and by far the most effective in history.[7] The general strike in Nicaragua was much shorter and less effective, but there is no doubt the political conflict was at least as important as the armed struggle.[8] While this urban character does not necessarily invalidate peasant-based theories of revolution, it does bring up a question about their applicability.

Third, both of these revolutions raise the possibility that ideas must be given more attention than accorded by recent theories. Liberation theology and Islamic activism are both phenomena pointing to the importance of human will in bringing about desired results. Yet Skocpol has been particularly emphatic in rejecting a voluntarist interpretation and emphasizing the structural basis of revolutions. In such a formulation, religious ideas or any other ideas are not decisive in moving people to revolutionary mobilization.

Besides the problems posed for Skocpol's theory, a comparative investigation of Iran and Nicaragua is interesting for another reason. From a broad comparative and historical perspective, these two revolutions were very similar in their causes and outcomes, as I show in the following chapters. Both revolutions were launched by the weakening of their respective modernizing, narrow, and military-based dictatorships, which were subject to economic and political pressures from abroad and from the domestic classes. Extensive mobilization of the urban poor played a decisive role. Finally, as predicted by Skocpol, personalistic, autocratic regimes gave way to more bureaucratic, centralized, and mass-mobilizing regimes run by new political elites. Nevertheless, as both of these revolutions reached their decade mark, important contrasts in outcomes—in both official ideologies and the actual pattern of political, cultural, and socioeconomic organization—continued to be apparent. This study attempts to explain the similarities and differences in outcomes. Throughout this work, the guiding question is whether or not the insights generated by recent studies on revolutions in general and Skocpol's argument in particular, which attempt to explain the breakdown of agrarian protobureaucracies, are sufficient for explaining the disintegration of dictatorships situated within the context of peripheral formations.[9]

To answer this question, I begin with a close look at Skocpol's explanatory framework. Objections can be raised regarding the methodological soundness of an endeavor that begins with the critique and modifications of only one theoretical perspective. I, however, continue to dwell on Skocpol's analysis because of its special character. Her comparative analysis of revolutions was informed by an in-depth examination of a multitude of theories about states, international factors, and peasant communities. Furthermore, her book has helped generate an important body of literature that in many ways goes beyond her contribution and sheds light on revolutionary outcomes, the relationship between capitalism and revolution, and the role of ideology, to name a few.[10] In this study, I draw freely from the useful insights of the literature that informed, and was informed by, her work. I also draw on the literature not normally associated with theories of revolution—e.g., urbanization in peripheral formations. I have, nevertheless, found it useful to maintain Skocpol's *States and Social Revolutions* as the focal point against which, in the three areas mentioned above, I can play my ideas and from which I can be directed toward areas where some tentative answers may be found. In the rest of this chapter, I tease out that which is potentially applicable in her argument and utilize theoretical insights developed by others to explain certain phenomena her analysis cannot.[11]

Skocpol and Social Revolutions

Skocpol begins her analysis with methodological advice. She suggests social revolutions are complex phenomena and cannot be explained simply by specifying the causal dynamics of one factor. Rather, she insists causation is a matter of "conjunctural, unfolding interactions of originally separately determined processes."[12] This conjunctural approach leads her to reject an intentionalist/voluntarist interpretation. Ideas and intentions are not decisive in moving people to revolutionary mobilization. Revolutions are not made as revolutionaries would have us believe; they merely happen as a result of the coincidence of several causal processes.

Her depiction of these causal processes is based on a simple premise: the crucial trigger for social revolutions in modernizing agrarian bureaucracies is the incapacitation of administrative and military machineries. This is not a particularly controversial assertion. Skocpol's contribution is her delineation of the precise processes leading to this administrative paralysis. The crux of her argument rests on the notion that political elites occupying state institutions can exert a significant *autonomous* role vis-à-vis the economically dominant classes. This allows her to conceptualize the project of state-building as competition against influential domestic actors as well other as state-builders within the international state system. In this competition, it is not only that state institutions have an "underlying integrity and logic of their own" or that the state personnel can pursue their own specific interests.[13] Skocpol's controversial contribution is her denotation of autonomy as state actions for ends that are opposed to "immediate" interests and, to a considerable extent, the "fundamental" interests of the dominant class.[14] This kind of action has the potential of causing basic structural change through which the existing mode of production, and its dominant class, would be supplanted by a new one. Presumably, this was precisely what occurred in Japan's "revolution from above."[15]

If, however, the potentially autonomous state is caught in a situation in which it is forced to respond to contradictory pressures coming simultaneously from the internally dominant class and foreign competitors, then a different possibility emerges. Since the state is overextended and poorly organized for military undertakings, its continuous effort to keep up with the more powerful states leads to the increasing possibility of military and fiscal crisis. Faced with this possibility, the state seeks to strengthen itself through reforms or mobilizing more economic resources, such as ending tax privileges for the rich or gaining direct control of agricultural surplus. However, when the propertied classes have political leverage within and against the administrative machinery of monarchical bureaucracies, as in prerevolutionary China and France, they can block autocratic attempts at reforms intended to increase the state's capacity to compete with stronger states. The resultant conflict can immobilize the repressive and administrative apparatus and ultimately lead to its breakdown.[16]

This administrative and military breakdown, in turn, opens the way for widespread popular revolts that erupt precisely because they can take advantage of the hiatus of governmental supervision and sanctions. Not all popular revolts constitute successful and irreversible attacks against the basic structural arrangements of society. In agrarian bureaucracies, Skocpol argues, only peasants having some institutionally based collective solidarity and autonomy from direct day-to-day supervision and control by landlords are capable of self-initiated rebellion against landlords and the state (as in France and Russia). In China, where the gentry controlled much of village life, the revolutionary process took much longer, and peasant revolts could not occur until the Communist party started to mobilize the population.

Once the state has been weakened and peasant uprisings have occurred, the main activity of revolution is the reconsolidation of state power by political leaders who come "from the ranks of educated marginal elites oriented to state employments and activities."[17] Here, once again, she makes an argument for looking at the activities of revolutionary leaders and not their ideologies or social origins. At the same time, she looks at revolutionary outcomes in terms of a stronger, more bureaucratic, and more highly centralized state. This is because only a regime that can abolish the special privileges of the landed class, free up resources, and provide the administrative machinery to utilize them will be able to consolidate power in the postrevolutionary period.

Clearly, Skocpol's specific explanatory hypotheses cannot be used directly to analyze the Iranian and Nicaraguan revolutions. Iran and Nicaragua were not agrarian bureaucracies, and peasants did not constitute the major insurrectionary force. Nonetheless, her conjunctural and nonintentionalist approach is helpful because it suggests a focus on the "nexes of state/state, state/economy, and state/class relationships" to understand the old regime's vulnerabilities.[18] In this study, I follow her advice by discussing the institutional characteristics of prerevolutionary states in Iran and Nicaragua and their special vulnerabilities in relation to domestic classes and foreign actors. I build my analysis on Skocpol's general discussion of state autonomy, showing how the disintegration of a potentially autonomous state in the face of pressures from international and domestic forces launches a revolution. However, I also propose modifications in her explanatory hypotheses to make them applicable to more recent revolutionary examples. More specifically, I argue that her analysis can become more pertinent to the contemporary world by:

1. locating her analysis in the changing balance of class forces occasioned by uneven development of capitalism on a world scale. This

kind of analysis will allow us (a) to develop an understanding of the internal dynamics of states in peripheral formations and the kinds of internal and external restraints imposed on them, and (b) to explain the changing coalescence of oppositional groupings, in particular to explicate the declining influence of the peasantry as the "dynamite" of revolutionary process and the increasing influence of intermediate classes in the launching as well as the processes of revolutions.

2. introducing a broader understanding of ideology to account for the importance of ideas, actions, or interests (both religious and secular) in the processes of the two contemporary revolutions.[19]

Uneven Development and State Autonomy

In what ways is the character of the peripheral state shaped by the position it holds in the global political economy? The answer to this question must begin with an understanding of the role of states in general. In this study, the state is defined as an entity analytically separable from the class structure. This is not to say one can understand any political regime without relating it to the structure of accumulation; it is merely to observe a certain degree of indeterminacy in this relationship. This means the state has a certain internal dynamic and momentum of its own, with a personnel that attempts to preserve itself and its positions. To understand this internal dynamic, it is important first to conceptualize the state as a set of institutions and bodies comprising the government (composed of various branches, levels, etc.) and military and internal security apparatuses. The state also includes regulatory agencies operating in the economy and "enterprises established, controlled and formally owned or financed by the government which produce commodities or provide non-commodified goods or services."[20] Clearly, the concentration of coercive power in the military/police apparatus makes the state a formidable means of domination for those who control it. It is also important to note that the constitutive elements of the state include both the state apparatus (civil and military bureaucracies) and those having formal control over this apparatus.[21] This is why it is important to decipher not only the institutional makeup of the state and the conflicting interests that constitute it but also "the actor, or set of actors, who promulgates and enforces the laws of a society, of which most important are those governing property rights."[22]

Viewed in this way, the state can develop interests *contrary* to the interests of economically important classes in the society. These interests operate on two levels: institutional and individual. On the institutional level, these interests are derived from the quest for institutional preservation and perpetuation. The pursuit of order, power, and resources should be conceived in these terms. On the individual level, these interests are derived from the desire to maximize wealth and power. Even if wealth and power are only a means to something else—e.g., gaining prestige, advancing an ideological position, preserving the status quo, avoiding trouble—they are necessary for achieving other goals.[23]

The existence of distinct and even contradictory interests, however, does not mean that the state or state rulers will necessarily be able to exercise autonomy in pursuing their interests. There are many external and internal constraints on this autonomy. Internally, although the pursuit of self-preservation is a general organizational interest, the state may not be unified on how to achieve this goal. Furthermore, leading individuals within the state apparatus also have interests that at any particular moment may be at variance with the general organizational interest. Internal fragmentation due to either of these two reasons inhibits autonomy because the conception of what precisely constitutes the state's interest becomes muddled. But, in states where one ruler clearly dominates—prerevolutionary Iran and Nicaragua—the possibility of autonomy is enhanced since it is very clear the state's interest lies in formulating policies that would maximize the ruler's objectives: wealth and power.[24]

A clear conception of an interest, however, does not necessarily lead to its actualization. For instance, a virtual monopoly over coercive power does not necessarily mean a perfect monitoring ability. Thus, policies intended to enhance the ruler's interests may not lead to the desired results because of the state agents' desire (and ability) to enhance their own personal goals as opposed to the ruler's. This is why it is important to examine the extent to which state agents conform to formal, rational rules on which the bureaucracy rests. If they are amenable to giving preference to certain class interests in exchange for financial rewards, state autonomy is undermined and the influence of the group able to purchase favors is enhanced. An examination of actual autonomy must therefore entail an elaboration of the following: (1) the locus of power (is it widespread or concentrated), (2) the conflicting interests existing within the state and their relative power capabilities, and (3) the ability of state institutions to pursue promulgated goals of the interests with the highest power capabilities.

The second set of constraints on state autonomy derives from the relationship between the state and the outside environment (both domestic and international). Internal constraints affect the way a state and state actors can deal with external actors and institutions; however, the power capabilities of external actors are also constraints on the actualization of state autonomy. In other words, the relative strength of various classes and class fractions, the degree of their internal cohesion, and their capacity to pressure for the satisfaction of their interests affect the type of policy that is formulated. In general, these constraints are related to how much the state depends on outside actors for resources.

In the first place, consideration must be given to the state's dependence on resources generated by private capital. The discussion of this dependence is more complicated in relation to peripheral formations since foreign capital is such a potent factor. Clearly, state policy will always favor those on whom the state depends. It is reasonable to hypothesize, for instance, that the greater the dependency of the state on private capital, the greater the potential for control over state policy by this element and therefore the less the state's autonomy. The same holds true for foreign capital, since it is always accompanied by the threat of investment withdrawal if state policy is not favorable to its needs and interests. This dependence becomes even more acute if the state's revenues are more or less based on one or two industries or agroexports and therefore heavily dependent on a fraction of capital, whether local or foreign.

Second, the extent to which a class is unified in its attempts to influence government through formal means (lobbying, routine consultation, participation in legislative bodies) or informal means (noncompliance with policy prescriptions, individual or group contacts with state personnel) must be investigated. Generally, "the greater the consolidated pressure of a class, particularly when combined with its formal exertion of pressure, the less the state's autonomy."[25]

In many peripheral formations, when state autonomy is measured only in relation to internal classes, there is no doubt that it is considerably high. Many observers have pointed out that, while states can be shaped, produced, and determined by class interests and action, they can also produce and transform classes and may even make them disappear through appropriate state policy.[26] For instance, empirical analyses have shown that local industrialists have neither the economic nor political characteristics to retain the progressive role of the bourgeoisie.[27] Moreover, studies of the bourgeoisie's self-perception in peripheral societies confirm that the bourgeoisie also lacks a "vocation for hegemony" or a national project, perceiving itself instead as politically subordinate to the state apparatus.[28]

In addition to the historical weakness of peripheral bourgeoisies, the expanded role of the peripheral state in the productive process has also enhanced state autonomy. It has been argued that the state in peripheral formations operates as a major capitalist enterprise in the sense of directly creating surplus value.[29] This means it is also interested in controlling labor, maximizing profit, and securing privileged use of resources for its personnel. This privileged use is influenced not only by private benefits for those in charge of specific programs but also by those collective demands of sections of the state apparatus—the military being the most notorious—which have a vested interest in channeling public funds into projects that serve their interest, often to the detriment of the economy as a whole.

Given the importance of the state in the process of class formation and its entrepreneurial role, state autonomy is clearly enhanced within the context of peripheral formations. This, however, immediately begs the question of autonomy from whom. The answer is that this autonomy is generally expressed vis-à-vis the internal classes—specifically the local bourgeoisie. Autonomy in relation to international capital is a bit more complicated since it entails the constraints of the world market. The extreme dependency position, as well as the world-system approach of Immanuel Wallerstein, sees little freedom of movement on the part of the state when it is faced with the requirements and demands of the world market. This position implies too much economic determinism. A much more reasonable approach has been enunciated by Hamza Alavi. He uses the notion of "structural imperative" to understand degrees of freedom (or restraints) and deviations from the requirements and demands of international capital in the workings of states under peripheral capitalism:

> The "structural imperative" refers to the basis of economic calculation in a capitalist society and the conditions that govern their outcome, both at the level of individual enterprise and the level of state. It defines the conditions of profitable economic behavior and the allocation of resources, delineates "efficient" from "inefficient" allocation with reference to performance on the market, and draws a line between solvency and insolvency. . . . But the notion of "structural imperative" does not mean that it determines in advance actions of individual capitalists or those of the capitalist state, as if they were perfectly programmed—as implied in the conception of capitalist state in functionalist Marxism. Neither individual capitalists nor the guardians of the capitalist state possess perfect knowledge and foresight, and their calculations are always fraught with uncertainty. Firms after all do go bankrupt.[30]

In this sense, the structural imperative of international capitalism does not necessarily predetermine the actions of a peripheral state. Rather, "it determines the consequences of such actions"[31] in such a way that actions against the logic of capitalism cannot continue without negative consequences for the peripheral capitalist state. This, however, does not preclude the possibility of certain states' taking actions against the logic of capitalism. These actions include miscalculations as well as direct attacks against international capital.

Once the possibility of direct attack against international capital is admitted, the task becomes one of unraveling the source of, and the processes that lead to, this attack. Throughout this study, I maintain that the external appropriation of economic surplus makes the state the centerpiece of nationalist struggle. This is why any discussion of revolutionary upheavals in peripheral formations must begin with the state and its precise relationship to international capital. This entails a discussion of the state's dependence on, or independence from, the financial, technological, institutional, ideological, and military resources of the internationally dominant classes and states. Dependence on these resources does not necessarily preclude autonomy, but it certainly inhibits it.

Skocpol also insists on incorporating the "world-historical context" into her analysis of state disintegration and revolutionary outcome. However, she mainly focuses on the international state system. Through this conceptualization, she is fully able to appreciate the role of international competition in stimulating peripheral states to undertake politically difficult modernizing efforts, which often, in turn, serve to trigger a revolutionary crisis. Despite this contribution, her failure to give similar emphasis to the uneven development of capitalism on a world scale has unnecessarily limited her analysis. For example, one would have difficulty explaining the revolutions in Iran and Nicaragua in terms of military competition with other states in the international system. Understanding state breakdown becomes easier if one incorporates into her state-centered analysis the contradictions arising in peripheral societies from the difficulties of simultaneously serving nationalist interests and sentiments and responding to the necessities of accumulation outside the territorial borders. It sheds light on the difficult predicament the peripheral states face in their attempts to portray themselves as the representatives of national interests.[32]

The inferior economic position of peripheral states, as well as their consequent weakness in the international power configurations, is important in another way. Because of their weakness, peripheral states are particularly vulnerable to pressures emanating from the world context. According to Walter Goldfrank, these pressures, arising from factors completely independent of revolutionary events, create a "permissive world context" within which a revolution in the periphery can become actualized.[33] Despite appreciating Skocpol's incorporation of international competition, Goldfrank ultimately finds her analysis inadequate because it does not take into account the very weak position of peripheral states:

Perhaps because the cases she has treated are all states with great power ambitions if not great power status, she does not explicitly raise as a causal necessity favorable configurations of the world system as a whole and of the immediate international context. As one moves toward the present temporally and toward the periphery of the world system spatially, this condition becomes increasingly crucial. . . . The Cuban Revolution in our own day depended at first on the opinion within the U.S. and later on Cold War rivalry to sustain its momentum. And the Vietnamese Revolution is in part clearly a creation of determinate great power configurations: The displacement of the French by the Japanese and the former's attempt to reestablish sovereignty; the U.S. effort to stop the spread of communism, and the Soviet and Chinese capacities to thwart that effort.[34]

It is, of course, very difficult to delineate systematically the variety of favorable world conditions. Goldfrank has, however, proposed three possibilities that are useful: (1) the major powers' preoccupation with war and internal difficulties, (2) an antagonistic balance of international powers, and (3) greater outside support for the revolutionaries than for the old order. As will be shown later, not all of these are applicable to the Iranian and Nicaraguan revolutions. It is important, however, to locate these two revolutions within the context of post-Vietnam and post-Watergate U.S. foreign policy. It was not at all insignificant that the major power closely identified with both prerevolutionary regimes took at least an ambiguous position toward their survival.

Uneven Development, Class Structure, and Urban Mobilization

Much ink has been spilled to discuss the uneven development of capitalism on a world scale and its socioeconomic effects on peripheral formations. The continuing condition of backwardness has been debated, and valuable insights have been generated. My intention is not to echo these discussions but to bring out two effects of uneven development of capitalism that are directly linked to the question of revolution: the effects on the class structure and on urbanization.

Uneven Development and Class Structure

Notwithstanding claims to the contrary, most theories of revolution have been influenced by Marxian theory of change, which is premised on the clash of polar classes. To be sure, most scholars do not accept class struggle as the causal necessity posited by Marxian theory of change. But the polar categories emphasized by Marx keep reappearing in theories of revolution in different forms (e.g., dominant class vs. subordinate classes, rich vs. poor, lower vs. upper class, elites vs. masses). In Skocpol's explanatory scheme, revolutions are not launched by class opposition but by a split between the dominant class and the state, yet the category of dominant class is still retained. This category, following Marxian analysis, is premised on the existence of a social division of labor in which groups of people must enter into relations with each other in the very act of production. According to Guglielmo Carchedi, these relations "are *antagonistic* because they unite, in a tie of mutual existential dependence, two antagonistic poles defined, for example, as relations between owner/appropriator/ non-laborer and the nonowner/expropriator/laborer. They are *asymmetric* because in this dependence one aspect (e.g., the owner vis-à-vis the non-owner) is the principal (or determinant) one and the other is the secondary (or determined) one."[35]

This asymmetry arises from one group's almost exclusive possession of all means of social production, consumption, raw materials, and instruments of production (machines, factories). Minor disagreements notwithstanding, Marxian analysis posits the existence of an economically dominant class that by virtue of its economic position dominates and controls all aspects of social life. Furthermore, this dominant class must necessarily exercise state power to maintain and reproduce the existing mode of production and social formation. Marxists have disagreed about the extent, the exact nature, and the specific location of this domination, but their disagreements are still premised on the "propertied class" dominating the economy, society, and the state (hegemony) and the nonowning laborers or subordinated classes striving for counterdomination.

Explaining social change in terms of asymmetric competition between polar classes is not very useful for analyzing peripheral social formations in which these polar classes are comparatively weak. It is more useful to understand that the uneven development of the capitalist mode of production in different regions and the consequent role of states as agents of class formation open a wide social space between these two polar classes. Antonio Gramsci identified this wide social space as "intermediate classes" and argued that, in some cases, they seek to carry on policies of their own and create ideologies that often influence broad strata of the society. In other words, these classes, which might include, for instance, the professional petty bourgeoisie and small-scale manufacturers, at times strive to achieve dominance/hegemony over subordinate classes and in the process generate appropriate ideologies to increase class organization and establish hegemony over other classes.[36]

Aijaz Ahmad, in a recent analysis of intermediate classes, goes beyond Gramsci and argues that the attempt to seek dominance is not limited to civil society but may, at times, involve an attempt to monopolize the state apparatus itself. Ahmad further argues that the intermediate classes try to exercise "dominance not only over the proletariat and peasantry but over the fundamental propertied classes as well."[37] Ahmad's restatement of Gramsci's analysis presents an important conceptual tool to analyze revolutions in the periphery. A lengthier quotation can give a better understanding of what Ahmad proposes:

> Classes exist as historical actors in so far as they struggle against other classes, and struggle is often for dominance. The intermediate classes are not passive bearers who merely serve the interests of other classes. Rather, like the polar classes, they too form multi-class alliances. In accordance with the actual balance of class powers obtaining in particular conjunctures, these intermediate classes may well accept, provisionally or for entire historical epochs, the leadership of a more powerful class. However, these political strategies and political restrictions do not imply that an intermediate class foregoes that which is constitutive of the existence of a class as such, namely the struggle for dominance over other classes.[38]

This line of analysis suggests that, in social formations with weak polar classes, the intermediate classes, normally led by the petty bourgeoisie, have the potential to rise to *prominence* in the field of politics. Accordingly, any analysis of revolution in such formations must examine the practices of these classes.

Urbanization as the Basis of Revolutionary Resistance

Urban mobilization as the basis of revolutionary resistance has received scant scholarly attention, which should not be surprising.[39] Peasant communities have been the major instigators of social change in "classic" revolutions and in the overwhelming majority of communist-inspired or nationalist revolutions of the twentieth century. Accordingly, many hypotheses have been developed to explain factors affecting the nature and existence of peasant revolutionary activities.[40] For the sake of this analysis, what is important is the utility of these hypotheses in explaining revolutionary activity within urban communities—a question that has arisen with the increasing urbanization of peripheral formations.

In her analysis of the Iranian Revolution, Skocpol suggests that two concepts, developed in *States and Social Revolutions* to explain revolutionary activity within peasant communities, can be transferred to poor urban communities: solidarity and autonomy.[41] Thus, in the case of Iran, opposition to the shah was made possible by the existence of autonomous, urban communal enclaves connected to the traditional centers of petty-commodity production and the religious networks embedded in them.

Although this analysis can give us clues about revolutionary processes, it cannot explain everything. In both Nicaragua and Iran, popular resistance had multiple social origins and organizational expressions. The structural conditions inherent in poor urban communities can help explain the pattern of mobilization among the urban poor, but it cannot explain the multiclass nature of these revolutions and the way bonds were forged across classes. For that, we also need to look at the structure of the urban community as a whole and its relationship to the state.

Given the central role of the state in the industrialization processes of most peripheral formations, it is only logical to assume that political conflict increasingly takes the form of interaction between the state and organized urban groupings. This is because, in the urban setting, all classes demand access to the collective material condition of daily life, and the state increasingly intervenes to resolve or ameliorate the contradictions arising from these conflicting demands. This "politicizes the totality of urban contradictions, transforms the state into a manager of the means of daily life."[42] Urban antagonisms, unlike rural conflicts that are generally between polar classes, thus become conflicts between the urban classes and the state, which mediates and manages class relations in the cities. In other words, the overwhelming power the state acquires in the urban context creates the potential for the creation of a multiclass negative coalition that can be mobilized to transform the state.[43]

During ordinary periods in peripheral cities, popular organizations aimed at improved social relations for subordinate classes are generally closely allied with, if not controlled by, state bureaucracies.[44] In revolutionary situations, however, the state loses its ability to continue its clientelist relationships with these organizations, and important bonds are forged between subordinate classes and organizations linked to other social groupings. It is within this context that preexisting social bonds and the organizational potential existing in the poor urban communities (long established or more recent) become important and decisive. The weakening of the state allows for the loosening of methods developed to control potentially volatile popular sectors. This, in turn, eases the transformation of friendship and kinship networks, as well as neighborhood and religious organizations, into political organizations or opens the way for strategic alliances among external organizations operating within the poor urban settlements. The investigation of preexisting social bonds is, therefore, important in two ways. First, it allows us to understand revolutionary processes—i.e., exactly how resources are mobilized to confront the state.[45] Second, it gives us clues about revolutionary outcomes. Although preexisting social bonds give prospective state-builders the necessary resources to gain control, they are not the only resources revolutionaries have at their disposal. The role of revolutionary ideology must also be investigated.

The Question of Ideology

How to conceptualize the role of ideology in revolutionary processes and outcomes is highly contested. Skocpol, I think correctly, rejects the influence of "idea systems deployed as self-conscious political arguments by identifiable political actors."[46] Yet, in her attempt to combat the "purposive image," she goes too far. From the correct notion that "innovative revolutionary propaganda retailed to the masses overnight"[47] does not determine revolutionary processes and outcomes, she deduces the much more sweeping generalization that ideas, actions, and interests do not matter, a logical leap that cannot be sustained. Even Skocpol's later attempts to deal with the importance of ideas in the French and Iranian revolutions are problematic. Her argument is based on a shaky compromise: the study of world views is justified only if it has long been in place (as in Iran and France) and has become part of what she calls "cultural idioms."[48] This uneasy compromise not only is problematic in the Iranian and French cases, because it does not take into account the dynamic nature of idea systems associated with these revolutions, but also points to the conceptual difficulty that exists in *States and Social Revolutions.*[49]

The problem partly arises from Skocpol's identification of ideology as a purely subjective condition that is presumably articulated by revolutionary leaders to inspire the masses to rebel. This definition is simply too narrow. In this study, I prefer a broader definition that goes beyond pure subjectivity and sees ideologies/world views as cognitive processes shaping, and shaped by, the real actions of human beings. Approached in this manner, world views do matter in the sense that they are responses to, and producers of, changing social and economic conditions. As such, they appeal to the cognitive processes of individuals responding to their immediate conditions and, under revolutionary situations, hoping to effect fundamental changes in the sociopolitical system.

Ideologies also matter on a much broader level of culture. As Gramsci pointed out a long time ago, domination is reflected and mediated through culture. This means that cultural practices, orientations, meaning systems, and social outlooks as well as explicit ideological systems of the dominant class are diffused throughout civil society. Given the weakness of peripheral bourgeoisies, however, the extent to which the subordinate classes incorporate this dominant value system may be limited.[50] This is especially noticeable when the upper and intermediate classes begin consuming fashions, customs, ideas, and educational methods to which the subordinate classes do not have access. In these circumstances, the subordinate classes' reaction to domination can take the form of completely distinct value systems that not only reject the prevalent inequalities but also differentiate them from other classes by repudiating everything with which the dominant ideology is identified. Religion can be a source of this alternative value system since it offers at least a framework for alternative interpretations of the social setting. This is especially possible if, as some have argued, urban capitalist relations do not necessarily lead to secularization, as generally presumed by earlier modernization theories. In other words, rather than disintegrating, religion can become a strategy for coping with the changes brought about in people's social networks by industrialization and urbanization.[51]

Of course, the development of alternative value systems does not happen overnight, and its occurrence is very much dependent on the nature of the dominant value system. It is often the case that subordinate value systems promote accommodative responses to inequality.[52] However, they may sometimes promote a radical oppositional interpretation of class inequality. The major question is how this transformation occurs. This question can only be answered through concrete historical analysis—a task to which chapter 4 is devoted.

NOTES

1. The use of "new" orientation is perhaps a misnomer since many of the recent works are heavily indebted to two seminal works on revolution that came out in the 1960s: B. Moore, Jr., *Social Origins of Dictatorship and Democracy* (Boston: Beacon Press, 1966), and E. R. Wolf, *Peasant Wars of the Twentieth Century* (New York: Harper & Row, 1969). Both of these works, in fact, have the same orientation as later works. I, however, feel justified in suggesting a new orientation since the literature on revolution did not incorporate the ideas developed by Moore and Wolf until more recently. In the interim, the social scientific theories of revolution were less historical and more intent on developing *general* theories about why and when revolutionary situations arise. As such, they were grounded in fairly well-developed theories of social behavior drawn from psychology, sociology, and political science. For an excellent analysis of the shift to the new orientation, see J. Goldstone, "Theories of Revolution: The Third Generation," *World Politics* 32 (April 1980), pp. 425–53. For examples of the new orientation, see J. Paige, *Agrarian Revolution* (New York: Free Press, 1975); E. K. Trimberger, *Revolutions from Above* (New Brunswick, N.J.: Transaction Books, 1978); S. N. Eisenstadt, *Revolution and the Transformation of Societies* (New York: Free Press, 1978); W. L. Goldfrank, "Theories of Revolution and Revolution without Theory: The Case of Mexico," *Theory and Society* 7 (Jan.–March

1979), pp. 97–134; T. Skocpol, *States and Social Revolutions: A Comparative Analysis of France, Russia and China* (Cambridge: Cambridge University Press, 1979); J. Walton, *Reluctant Rebels* (New York: Columbia University Press, 1984); and J. A. Goldstone, *Revolutions* (San Diego: Harcourt Brace Jovanovich, 1986).

2. The proponents of the historical grounding of sociopolitical theory essentially explain the term as being embedded in time. According to Charles Tilly, it means "focused on some historically specific setting or process. Being grounded in history clearly prevents these theories from being applied over time and place without any adjustments. However, these theories do develop hypotheses that are helpful in guiding research." C. Tilly, *As Sociology Meets History* (New York: Academic Press, 1981), p. 26.

3. In particular, see Goldfrank, "Theories of Revolution," and Walton, *Reluctant Rebels*.

4. In her article, "Rentier State and Shi'a Islam in the Iranian Revolution," *Theory and Society* 11 (May 1982), pp. 265–304, Skocpol also lays out three problems the Iranian case poses for her structural approach: (1) the apparent influence of modernization, (2) the voluntarist tendencies of the revolution, and (3) the lack of pressure from abroad. The variations I have proposed are similar to hers but are a bit more general. For instance, she sees lack of foreign pressure as a major variation. I find the way the Iranian state collapsed as problematic, given the lack of foreign pressure and fiscal crisis. I do not find her concern over the "seeming influence of modernization" to be justified since, as she cogently pointed out in her book, all revolutions *seem* to have been caused by modernization. Yet her thorough formulation showed why modernization is not really a sufficient cause. The urban nature of the Iranian Revolution is, however, an important variation and is related to modernization. As such, it must be dealt with. Finally, my concern over voluntarism is the same as hers.

5. The percent of urban population compared to total population was in Nicaragua, 54 percent in 1980; Iran, 50 percent in 1980; China, 10 percent in 1953; and Vietnam, 15 percent in 1960. In addition, the makeup of the labor force was significantly different in Iran and Nicaragua, and literacy rates were higher. For instance, the percentage of labor force in agriculture was 44 percent in Nicaragua (1978), 40 percent in Iran (1978), 81 percent in Vietnam (1960), and 69 percent in China (1950). Literacy rates were as follows: Nicaragua, 57 percent in 1977; Iran, 50 percent in 1977; China, 10 percent in 1949; and Vietnam, 18 percent in 1950. The latter two figures are generally used to assess the extent of socioeconomic development. Iran and Nicaragua clearly did have economic growth in some areas. But, as in most Third World countries, urbanization did not necessarily mean industrialization since many of those in the urban areas (especially in Nicaragua) were either marginally employed or involved in petty-commodity production and trade. Sources are the World Bank, *World Development Report, 1980* (Washington, D.C.: The World Bank, 1980), and R. H. Dix, "The Varieties of Revolution," *Comparative Politics* 15, 3 (1983), pp. 281–94.

6. The forces of the Sandinista National Liberation Front reportedly numbered fewer than 1,000 — largely university dropouts.

7. Iran actually yielded a textbook example of the general strike as a primary weapon in the revolutionary seizure of power. Massive street demonstrations also manifested the political bent of confrontation. As Fred Halliday points out, the demonstrations in the last months, which involved up to two million people in Tehran and several million more in the provincial towns, were unprecedented in the oppositional context. F. Halliday, "The Iranian Revolution: Uneven Development and Religious Populism," *Journal of International Affairs* 36 (Fall/Winter 1982–83), pp. 186–207.

8. On this, see R. Chavarria, "The Nicaraguan Insurrection," in *Nicaragua in Revolution*, ed. Thomas W. Walker (New York: Praeger, 1982), pp. 25–40.

9. The term *peripheral formations* is intended to pertain to countries that, unlike core/center capitalist countries, are characterized by *disarticulation* between economic sectors. Since most of the industries producing means of production are absent, the links between departments I and II (producing means of production and consumer goods respectively) analyzed by Marx in his schemes of reproduction, while existing on the global level, are incomplete within these countries. On this, see S. Amin, *Accumulation on a World Scale* (New York: Monthly Review Press, 1974).

10. For a brief review of recent endeavors, see Jack Goldstone's review of the study of revolution in the *Newsletter of the Historical and Comparative Section of the American Sociological Association* (April 1986). See also Goldstone, *Revolutions.*

11. It is important to point out that Skocpol never claims the scheme she lays out in *States and Social Revolutions* can be directly applied to other cases. A historical approach, by definition, prohibits application over time and place without adjustments. The concern in this project, however, is whether adjustments are enough or theoretical rethinking is also necessary.

12. Skocpol, *States and Social Revolutions*, p. 320, n. 16.

13. Ibid., p. 27.

14. The distinction between immediate and fundamental interests is taken from E. O. Wright, *Class, Crisis, and the State* (London: New Left Books, 1978), pp. 88–102. According to Wright, "Immediate class interests constitute interests within a given class structure of social relations; fundamental interests center on interests which call into question the structure of social relations itself." Ibid., p. 89.

15. See Moore, *Social Origins*, p. 299; Trimberger, *Revolutions from Above*; and T. Skocpol and E. K. Trimberger, "Revolutions and the World-Historical Development of Capitalism," in *Social Change in Capitalist World Economy*, ed. B. H. Kaplan (Beverly Hills, Calif.: Sage, 1978), pp. 123–24.

16. In the Russian case, the landed nobility was not as obstructive as in the French and Chinese cases. However, the international pressures associated with World War I were much greater.

17. Skocpol, *States and Social Revolutions*, p. 167.

18. Ibid., p. 292.

19. The general suggestions introduced here are very much influenced by

Michael Burawoy's criticism of Skocpol. M. Burawoy, "State and Social Revolution in South Africa," *Kapitalistate* 9 (1981), pp. 93–122.

20. C. L. Baylies, *"The State and Class Formation in Zambia"* (Ph.D. thesis, Department of Sociology, University of Wisconsin, 1978), p. 4.

21. N. Hamilton, *Limits of State Autonomy: Post-Revolutionary Mexico* (Princeton, N.J.: Princeton University Press, 1982). This definition is derived from both Max Weber and Friedrich Engels. Engels and Weber seem to agree on the constitution of the state. The main difference lies in Weber's insistence that it is only the modern state that monopolizes legitimate force.

22. M. Levi, "The Predatory Theory of Rule," *Politics and Society* 10, 4 (1981), p. 438. As will become obvious below, I have been very much influenced by Levi's work. Unlike Skocpol, whose main concern is to lay out "macroconstraints" on state policy, Levi insists that a theory of rule is possible only when micro and macro approaches are combined. Accordingly, she calls for a deciphering of the "microfoundations" (i.e., the concrete interests that lay behind different state policies) of macro questions.

23. Ibid.

24. Ibid.

25. Baylies, "The State and Class Formation in Zambia," p. 18.

26. P. Evans, *Dependent Development: The Alliance of Multinationals, State and Local Capital in Brazil* (Princeton, N.J.: Princeton University Press, 1979); Hamilton, *Limits of State Autonomy.*

27. See, for instance, F. H. Cardoso and E. Faletto, *Dependency and Development in Latin America* (Berkeley: University of California Press, 1979); Evans, *Dependent Development;* and G. Gereffi and P. Evans, "Transnational Corporations, Dependent Development and State Policy in the Semi-periphery: A Comparison of Brazil and Mexico," *Latin American Research Review* 16, 3 (1981), pp. 31–64.

28. P. McDonough, *Power and Ideology in Brazil* (Princeton, N.J.: Princeton University Press, 1981). For a discussion of this, see P. Evans, "Reinventing the Bourgeoisie: State Entrepreneurship and Class Formation in Dependent Capitalist Development," *American Journal of Sociology* 88, supplement (1982), pp. 210–47.

29. For an excellent review of the recent literature on the role of the state in the productive process (with an emphasis on Latin America), see W. L. Canak, "The Peripheral State Debate: State Capitalist and Bureaucratic Authoritarian Regimes in Latin America," *Latin American Research Review* 19, 1 (1984), pp. 3–36.

30. H. Alavi, "State and Class under Peripheral Capitalism," in *Introduction to the Sociology of Developing Societies,* ed. H. Alavi and T. Shanin (New York: Monthly Review Press, 1982), p. 294.

31. Ibid.

32. Class analysis has not been very successful at incorporating the tensions between nationalism and uneven development of capitalism on a world scale. John Ehrenreich argues that this difficulty in Marxian class analysis arises from Marx's own misunderstanding of the proletariat, which prevented him from

foreseeing its heterogeneity and the emergence of intermediate strata. At a deeper level, by seeing history in terms of rationally determined (class) interests, Marxism has made itself poorly suited for "understanding nationalism, with its passionate romanticism, its mix of progressivism and traditionalism, and its cross-class appeal" (p. 4). Thus, it usually has been forced to relegate nationalism to an "inexplicable aberration" or "false consciousness." Ehrenreich argues that the regularity of nationalism warrants its conceptualization in terms of "a mode of resistance to disruptions created as capitalism penetrates" (p. 16). J. H. Ehrenreich, "Socialism, Nationalism and Capitalist Development," *Review of Radical Political Economics* 15 (Spring 1983), pp. 1–40. In a similar vein, Tom Nairn argues that nationalism can be understood as an attempt of a rising or weak bourgeoisie simultaneously to harness resources for the development of capitalism and to resist subordination to a powerful international bourgeoisie. To this end, the emergent capitalist class mobilizes the only resource at its disposal—the people. T. Nairn, "The Modern Janus," *New Left Review*, no. 94 (1975), pp. 3–29. The precise nature of the rendezvous between nationalism and capitalism and its effects on the Iranian and Nicaraguan states will be discussed in the case studies.

33. Goldfrank, "Theories of Revolution."

34. Ibid., pp. 148–49.

35. G. Carchedi, "Class Analysis and the Study of Social Forms," in *Beyond Method: Strategies for Social Research*, ed. G. Morgan (Beverly Hills, Calif.: Sage, 1983), p. 348.

36. A. Gramsci, *Selections from Political Writings: 1921–1926* (New York: International Publishers, 1978), p. 409. As will be discussed later, Gramsci's notion of ideology is different from Skocpol's. For Gramsci, it is not a purely subjective condition but a cognitive process that shapes, and is shaped by, the real actions of people in the real world.

37. A. Ahmad "Class, Nation, and State: Intermediate Classes in Peripheral Societies," in *Middle Classes in Dependent Countries*, ed. D. L. Johnson (Beverly Hills, Calif.: Sage, 1985), pp. 47–48.

38. Ibid., p. 48.

39. For important works on the issue of urban mobilization and revolution, see R. Dix, "The Varieties of Revolution," *Comparative Politics* 15, 3 (1983), pp. 281–94; R. Dix, "Why Revolutions Succeed and Fail," *Polity* 16, 3 (1984), pp. 423–46; and J. Gugler, "The Urban Character of Contemporary Revolutions," *Studies in Comparative and International Development* 17 (Summer 1982), pp. 60–73.

40. For a useful survey of exact differences among theories emphasizing the role of peasantry, see T. Skocpol, "What Makes Peasants Revolutionary?" *Comparative Politics* 14, 3 (1982), pp. 265–304.

41. T. Skocpol, "Rentier State and Shi'a Islam."

42. M. Castells, *The Urban Question: A Marxist Approach* (Cambridge, Mass.: MIT Press, 1977), pp. 42–43.

43. Following this logic, it is conceivable that despite rapid and basic transformation of the state, accompanied and in part carried through by class-

based revolts from below, no changes in the class structure occur because the kind of industrialization occurring in the periphery makes the state omnipresent in every aspect of urban life and thus responsible for all its problems. Of course, widespread mobilization against the state always has the potential to transform the social structure radically. This occurs when the multiclass coalition begins to unravel and a particular group of revolutionaries pursues radical policies to cement its hold over the state. More on this in chapter 5.

44. W. Cornelius, Jr., *Politics and the Migrant Poor in Mexico City* (Palo Alto, Calif.: Stanford University Press, 1975); J. Walton, "Urban Political Movements and Revolutionary Change in the Third World," *Urban Affairs Quarterly* 15, 1 (1979), pp. 3–22.

45. As will be discussed in chapter 3, those communities that are closely knit and share a common culture are more easily mobilized. On this, see also C. J. Calhoun, "The Radicalism of Tradition and the Question of Class Struggle," in *Rationality and Revolution*, ed. M. Taylor (Cambridge: Cambridge University Press, 1988), pp. 129–75. Calhoun convincingly argues that traditional communities are important bases of radical mobilization because their integral "networks of kinship, friendship, share crafts, or recreations offer lines of communication and allegiance. People who live in well-integrated communities do not need elaborate formal organization in order to mount a protest. They know, moreover, whom to trust and whom not to trust. Communal relations are themselves important resources to be 'mobilized' for any insurgency." Ibid., p. 149.

46. T. Skocpol, "Cultural Idioms and Political Ideologies in the Reconstruction of State Power: A Rejoinder to Sewell," *Journal of Modern History* 57, 1 (1985), p. 91.

47. Skcopol, "Rentier State and Shi'a Islam," pp. 275–76.

48. Skocpol, "Cultural Idioms."

49. For a brilliant critique of Skocpol's position on ideology, see W. H. Sewell, "Ideologies and Social Revolutions: Reflections on the French Case," *Journal of Modern History* 57, 1 (1985), pp. 57–85. See also J. Dunn, *Rethinking Modern Political Theory* (Cambridge: Cambridge University Press, 1985), chapter 4.

50. R. G. Oliven, "Culture Rules OK: Class and Culture in Brazilian Cities," *International Journal of Urban and Regional Research* 3, 1 (1979), pp. 29–48.

51. For an example of this, see ibid., and F. Kazemi, *Poverty and Revolution in Iran: The Migrant Poor, Urban Marginality and Politics* (New York: New York University Press, 1980).

52. F. Parkin, *Class Inequality and Political Order* (New York: Praeger, 1971).

2

Peripheral State, Prominent Classes, and Revolution

They said that they were aiming at the creation of a modern
state . . . and they in fact produced a bastard.
                                        —Antonio Gramsci,
                                           The Prison Notebooks

The revolutions in Iran and Nicaragua occurred in societies situated
within an international arena dominated by the more economically integrated nations. Despite major differences in their political economies,
they manifested similar and classic symptoms associated with all peripheral societies: unemployment and underemployment, intersectoral imbalances, sprawling slums and squatter settlements in the cities, and the
separation of peasants from their means of production. Since most of the
economic and social factors arising from a disadvantaged economic
position are present in almost all peripheral formations, they cannot be
considered as the crucial trigger for these revolutions. The factor that
differentiated Iran and Nicaragua was the type of state that oversaw these
societies. Caught in the cross fire between nationalist sentiments and
external dependence and situated within a permissive world context,
these states, and the individual leaders who dominated them, proved
unable to maintain their hold over the society. The erosion of the coercive capabilities of these states, accelerated by certain immediate causes,
brought an explosion in the cities which, in the end, forced the individual
leaders to leave their countries. This, in turn, paved the way for further
sociopolitical radicalization. In this chapter, I lay out the dynamics of this
state breakdown, beginning with a history of state formations in Iran and
Nicaragua and then moving to a discussion of state structures and their
vulnerabilities. The interaction between these vulnerable states and their
respective economies and class structures is analyzed in the next section.

The chapter concludes with a discussion of the revolutionary conjuncture and remarks about similarities and differences in the nature of state breakdown in Iran and Nicaragua.

The Rise and Consolidation of the Prerevolutionary States

The states consolidated under the personal rule of Mohammad Reza Shah and the Somoza family were based on three bulwarks of support: economic appeasement of political contenders, political repression, and U.S. military and financial assistance. These helped Iran and Nicaragua avoid some of the political instabilities associated with most peripheral societies and paved the path to economic growth. In the long run, however, these sources of strength produced their opposite. That is, at the crossroad of foreign and domestic pressures, the internal mechanisms of political and economic control failed precisely because these sources of support had made it unnecessary for the regimes to develop linkages required for their survival during crisis periods. Much of the answer to how this happened lies in the ways the Iranian and Nicaraguan prerevolutionary states were formed and consolidated.

State Formation

The beginning of the modern state structure in Iran can be traced to Reza Shah Pahlavi's rise to power in the 1920s.[1] According to Ervand Abrahamian, this state no longer rested "on the sands of tribal contingents and communal manipulations, but on three stone pillars of a standing army, a modern bureaucracy, and extensive court patronage."[2] Iran experienced its most concentrated period of political centralization and economic development during Reza Shah's fifteen-year reign (1926–41). His method of rule was based on coercion, buttressed by extensive court patronage. More important, he did not actively cultivate the support of any one class for his regime. Even his relationship to the landed class was marred by a combination of coercion and appeasement. He rewarded some with high governmental positions, while killing many others. He solidified the legal basis of private property, but he attacked the power of many large landowners and tribal chiefs and made himself the largest landowner in the country.[3]

In short, despite the lack of class bases, or perhaps because of it, he managed to dominate internal politics and set the stage for the entrenchment of the Pahlavi dynasty. However, as is common in Iranian politics, external politics unraveled his rule when he became caught in the great power rivalry occasioned by World War II. His attempt to remain neutral (or to flirt with the Germans, some would say) led to his forced abdication, masterminded by the British, and his son, Mohammad Reza, became the shah. The postwar task of rebuilding the economy and reasserting Pahlavi dominance was a formidable one. The Allied invasion had discredited the Pahlavi dynasty, and this had unleashed social forces, already brewing under Reza Shah's dictatorial rule, which were quite difficult for the young, inexperienced shah to control. The next thirteen years were marked by intense conflict, and its resolution became the cornerstone on which the shah's power came to rest.

At the center of conflict was the question of dominance over the state. The destruction of Reza Shah's autocracy had heralded opportunities for a variety of social forces contesting for power.[4] The spectrum of social forces ranged from those representing landlords and tribal magnates to a nationally based and highly ideological communist movement, committed to mass mobilization and spearheaded by the Moscow-oriented Tudeh party. The regime was also faced with a vociferous nationalist and constitutionalist movement, whose opposition was directed at the monarchy's monopoly of power and its relationship to foreign powers.[5] Lacking the mass base that characterized the Tudeh party, the nationalist and constitutionalist politicians created the National Front, a coalition of parties representing a variety of interests, and staged their fight from the Iranian Parliament (Majles).

The issue of the nationalization of the Anglo-Iranian Oil Company (AIOC) nicely epitomized concerns over nationalism and constitutionalism. The meager revenues the Iranian government received from the AIOC had always been a sore point. In addition, the shah's refusal to challenge Britain on the oil issue created a platform from which to attack his increasing power. The confrontation between the Majles and the shah led to the prime ministership of the leader of the oil protest movement, Mohammad Mossadeq, and the nationalization of the oil industry a few months later. This act, however, brought the closing of the oil refinery, the withdrawal of all British technicians, an embargo on parts and equipment needed to maintain oil facilities, and an almost universal shipping boycott of Iranian oil. As the fiscal situation deteriorated, Mossadeq found it difficult to keep his National Front coalition together. Ultimately, he was overthrown by "a coalition of forces within and outside Iran—just as the Constitutional Revolution had been."[6]

On the most general level, Mossadeq's ouster was likely, given the context of the structural imperative of peripheral capitalism. As the head of the Iranian state, Mossadeq could nationalize a British company, but the AIOC could easily retaliate by gathering support from all other oil companies for a boycott of Iranian oil, which caused economic dislocations that severely penalized Mossadeq's government. Not surprisingly, the international boycott was terminated once the Iranian claim for full control was withdrawn by the reinstated Mohammad Reza Shah.[7]

Although the structural imperative set the stage for the downfall of Mossadeq, it was the internal conflict that ultimately undermined him. Mossadeq's social base had always been constructed on contradictory interests. The deteriorating economic conditions amplified their conflicts and weakened his original base of support. The major split was between the secular parties representing the modern intermediate class and parties representing the old petty bourgeoisie of the bazaars—centers of small commodity production and exchange in the urban areas—and led by religious leaders (ulama) traditionally connected to these centers. Disagreements led the parties representing the bazaar to defect. Mossadeq's relationship with the left also proved problematic. The nationalist forces had always had a tenuous relationship with the Tudeh party. While they both essentially agreed on their dislike of the royalty, they were clearly incompatible in their social bases and their vision of the future. Mutual suspicion led to inconsistent policies on the part of both sides. On the one hand, the Tudeh party became much more confrontational and, through its front organizations and affiliated unions, held mass meetings to demand higher wages and protest governmental restrictions. On the other hand, Mossadeq, while allowing the front organizations and demonstrations to continue, refused to form a broad alliance with the Tudeh against the royalist forces. Rejected by Mossadeq, the Tudeh failed to act against the U.S.-backed military coup to remove Mossadeq from power.[8]

The coup was a severe blow to both nationalist and communist forces as the reinstated shah pursued an effective campaign against them all. Ironically, the coalescence of contradictory interests to undermine a perceived antinationalist state had given rise to a much stronger state that owed its survival, at least partially, to foreign assistance. The U.S. government not only was implicated in the coup itself but had set the stage for the emergence of one-man rule in the years prior to Mossadeq's downfall.[9] Furthermore, it continued to remain the backbone of the regime, militarily and financially. By 1963, the shah's state emerged as an independent entity that completely dominated society. Empowered with a new, sophisticated secret police (SAVAK), he moved against all opposition. The Tudeh party was effectively neutralized, and a brief attempt by the bazaari classes and the religious community to prevent the shah's proposed reforms was crushed.[10] The state thus was able to shake itself loose of the conflicts within civil society. The shah's strategic conquest of the state precluded any particular class from controlling the state apparatus and represented complete state dominance in the economic and political spheres.

The situation in Nicaragua was a bit more complicated. More than any other part of the Central American isthmus, Nicaraguan society has been molded by the interaction of forces incorporating it into the world economic system and the peculiar political development it was forced to experience because of repeated foreign interventions.[11] The result has been a century of intense events marked by the intrusion of external forces into violently divisive internal politics, culminating in the 1979 insurrection. Foreign intervention, as one observer put it, not only "kept Nicaraguans fighting longer than they might have with only their own resources" but also "severely set back economic and political development."[12]

The roots of conflict can be traced to the country's independence from the Spanish empire. When the Spaniards quietly abandoned Central America in 1821, they left a power vacuum. Since Nicaragua did not have a traditional colonial economy geared to mining or agriculture, no powerful social group emerged to dominate civil society. In addition, since, during the colonial period, Central America was controlled through a weak administrative chain emanating from Guatemala City, political control decentralized around provincial towns. Limited commercialization reinforced the parochial rivalries of landlords and merchants, rendering their economic interests competitive rather than complementary. The result was factional politics centered around Nicaragua's two major cities: Granada and Leon.[13] The power struggle between the conservative Granadinos and the liberal Leonese was manipulated by foreigners, and this further inhibited the unification of the two regions.[14] Political rule vacillated between Liberal and Conservative parties, with the latter ultimately gaining the upper hand.

Despite regional conflict, had it not been for its geographic position, Nicaragua, like the rest of Central America, would have probably witnessed the emergence of a cohesive agrarian bourgeoisie associated with the rise of coffee as an export crop. Indeed, the agricultural base of the economy did bring a new class, which showed its desire to take control with the Liberal revolt led by José Santos Zelaya in 1893. Zelaya's presidency was literally Nicaragua's first national government. By forging internal cohesion, he opened the way for sixteen years of national development.

Ultimately, however, U.S. strategic interests thwarted the agroexporting bourgeoisie's desire for hegemony.[15] As is well known, the U.S. government seriously considered Nicaragua as a site for a transoceanic canal in the late nineteenth and early twentieth centuries. Accordingly, multiple U.S. interventions were staged either to ensure control over any future canal or to prevent competition for the canal in Panama.[16] These interventions cut short the Liberal revolution and created a largely autonomous state based on the Nicaraguan National Guard. According to Jeffrey Paige, this created conditions in which

> the National Guard, trained and initially paid and led by the United States, formed the core of a state that did not reflect the interests of the traditional landed oligarchy, the modernizing coffee bourgeoisie or even foreign capital. Its origins were strategic and military, not economic. In Guatemala, El Salvador, and Costa Rica, the state was simply the executive committee of the coffee planters' association; in Honduras it was the extension of American Banana companies. In Nicaragua it was a unit of the U.S. Marine Corps.[17]

The coffee bourgeoisie was not the only casualty. U.S. intervention and the resultant civil war between pro-U.S. and nationalist forces also impeded the modernization of agriculture. Later, the development of cotton export provided the impetus for a capitalist transformation of agricultural production, but, since the cotton bourgeoisie was divided between large growers and "small growers caught between exporters, pesticide firms, and the national bank," it was never able to "provide the cohesive nucleus for an export oligarchy of the kind that dominated Salvador or Guatemala."[18]

The person that successfully managed to assure the consolidation of the U.S.-supported state was Anastasio Somoza García. From his position as the commander of the National Guard, Somoza was able to take control of the presidency, put an end to the liberal-conservative bickering, and reserve political rule for his family for years to come.[19] Given the history of their rise to power, Somoza García and his sons always understood the vital role the United States played in their maintenance of political rule. To maintain this support, Somocistas strived to become one of the most faithful allies of the United States in Central America. Their loyalty was manifested in symbolic gestures in the United Nations and concrete actions, such as permission for the overt use of Nicaraguan territory by CIA agents and Guatemalan exiles to overthrow the government of Jacobo Arbenz in Guatemala.[20] An elaborate public relations/lobbying effort and close relations with U.S. policymakers —including a number of members of Congress during the 1970s— afforded Nicaragua direct access to the floors of Congress.[21] Of course, the Somoza family's efforts paid off as the U.S.-injected moral support and economic and military aid discouraged opponents of the regime, enriched the Somozas, and increased their capacity to coopt and repress their compatriots.[22] U.S. backing was seen by the upper and intermediate classes as evidence of the futility of any internally generated opposition.

State Structure

This brief historical overview suggests that the most important feature of the Iranian and Nicaraguan prerevolutionary states was their institutional detachment from the majority of the population. These states, which can be identified as personalist authoritarian, were distinguished by the nearly complete centralization of power and authority in the hands of individual leaders—Mohammad Reza Pahlavi and Anastasio Somoza Debayle. Like several other rulers who have fallen to revolutionary uprisings (e.g., Díaz in Mexico, Batista in Cuba, Duvalier in Haiti), the shah and Somoza controlled their respective states with iron fists and made linkages with other political contenders not to share power but only to ensure their continued domination. This combination of political and economic control made politics less complicated since decision making was institutionalized around these individual leaders. The politics of opposition was also simplified, because these leaders—along with their families, military, and sycophants—came to personify the state. This is why some observers have identified these states as patrimonial or neopatrimonial.[23]

The denotation of patrimonial domination is at least partially correct. Both these leaders not only were centers of decision making but also used classical patrimonial tactics—divide-and-rule and the creation of elaborate sets of overlapping and competing hierarchies, none of which was autonomous and all of which were dependent on them—to consolidate their power. This method of overlapping bureaucratic responsibilities was accompanied by an elaborate array of practices to intimidate and control military and civilian officials. In Iran, these included the appointment of antagonistic individuals as directors of major organizations within the government, surprise appointments, employment of shadow cabinets to follow the activities of an organization or ministry within the bureaucracy, and the reduction in stature of individuals who were too "smart" or "popular."[24] To ensure maximum dependence, corruption, which was tolerated and even encouraged, was used as a powerful means in, what one observer has called, "the seduction of the elite."[25]

To be sure, the Iranian state encompassed a very large bureaucracy, a sophisticated military, and an omnipresent security agency (SAVAK) that performed tasks ranging from economic management to torture. Their smooth functioning was indeed indispensable to the increasingly sophisticated Iranian economy and the more important international role Iran had developed. But decision making and communications within these organizations continued to move along vertical rather than horizontal lines. The military is a good case in point. In managing it, the shah maintained full control by checking promotions above the rank of major, according material privileges to the officer corps, juggling commands, and closing his eyes to corruption. Officers showing any signs of disloyalty were immediately removed. Several observers even report that, on occasion, disloyal officers, who had been given opportunities for graft, were purged under the guise of waging anticorruption campaigns.[26]

The result of all this was a military whose officer corps was deeply committed to the shah. Yet this personal commitment was secured at the expense of institutional commitment. Robert Graham argues that the denigration of the institutional commitment was necessitated by the role the armed services was intended to play in Iran: to be the ultimate defender of the throne.[27] From the shah's point of view, this role could only be performed if the military establishment itself were stripped of the potential to mount an attack against the throne. He thus set out to create, and to a large extent succeeded in creating, a large, unwieldy military establishment in which individual power bases were fragmented. This, of course, prohibited the possibility of independent and cohesive military action and in due time prevented the military from taking any action to protect its corporate identity. But it is also true that the military was expanded dramatically and professionalism was encouraged. The Iranian armed forces would not parallel the professionalism of their Chilean counterparts, but neither could they be placed in the category of Somoza's National Guard, whose only encouragement was graft and plunder.

In Nicaragua, the loyalty of the 7,500-strong National Guard, which was at once an army and a police force, was assured through a mixture of paternalism and corruption. According to Henri Weber, "The dictator served as the soldier's personal protector, a veritable regimental father."[28] He showed unwavering concern for members of the Guard. He even knew each officer personally and made sure they were taken care of financially. He went so far as to encourage guardsmen of all ranks to be corrupt, thus "isolating them psychologically from the people on whom they preyed and making them even more dependent on the Somoza family."[29] As the military extended its control over communications, internal revenues, railways, postal service, immigration, heath services, and prostitution, kickbacks became a way of life.[30] In addition, senior officers were routinely transferred to the state bureaucracy or a Somoza-controlled industry, where there was ample opportunity for personal enrichment. All this led to a convergence of interest between the Somozas and these hired men that was based on the maintenance of a sociopolitical order benefiting them both. This convergence of interest was further reinforced by the literal segregation of the Guard from the rest of the population. According to George Black, the Guard's privileged status gave them separate shops, schools, and hospitals; exclusive residential areas, like the suburbs of Las Colinas and Villa Fontana in the hills south of Managua; and subsidized food and clothing, including uniforms and boots produced in Somoza-owned factories.[31]

It is important to point out that the relationship with the Guard was not totally free of tensions and distrust. Like all dictators, the Somozas were haunted by the possibility of a coup d'etat. Accordingly, the National Guard was organized to foreclose such a possibility. Several examples given by Weber are important to point out since, as we shall see later, they can give important clues about the ineffectiveness of the Guard in dealing with a national insurgency:

> Guardia Colonels, who never had more than 300 or 400 men under their command, were systematically transferred at frequent intervals, so that they would not establish close links with their troops. The two elite units were entrusted to family members—one of them, the 2,500-strong and heavily armed Escuela de Entrenamiente Basico do Infanteria, being under the Command of Somoza's son, Anastasio 'Chiguin' Somoza Portocarrero. The Dictator consciously fanned rivalry among the higher officers. As a final precaution, combat units received only small reserves of ammunition.[32]

The civilian bureaucracies of these two countries manifested the same similarities and differences that existed in the militaries. Decision making was centralized in both countries, although the Iranian bureaucracy was much larger and perhaps more professional. In Nicaragua, the state was limited in scope, administratively fragmented, and corrupt. There were, of course, pockets of expertise centered around the Central Bank and several of the public enterprises in Nicaragua, such as the state-owned electrical company. This meant that economic policy could be coordinated through the Central Bank, but there was very little coherence within the rest of this fragmented administrative system, which employed an estimated 20,000 civil servants.[33]

The situation was a bit different in Iran because the bureaucracy was much larger.[34] The smooth functioning, no matter where the decisions were being made, was dependent on the technocrats who were running these institutions. At the top of the bureaucracy were individuals whose personal service was guaranteed through the coincidence of interest with the extant socioeconomic structure. That is, high-ranking state officials were given the opportunity to prosper "by sitting on managerial boards and facilitating lucrative government contracts."[35] The middle and lower ranks of the bureaucracy, however, did not develop into a source of solid support for the monarchy. Their loyalty was defined only by their relationship to the supreme patron rather than by more rational, bureaucratic ones. Furthermore, this relationship was generally bought through opportunities for social mobility opened by industrialization and the state use of oil revenues to expand bureaucratic employment. But the shah's personal dominance, which imposed restrictions on freedom of expression, elections, and the Majles, prevented members of the bureaucracy from becoming committed supporters of the shah, even when his economic and social policies suited their economic needs. Their lukewarm support for the monarchy was in keeping with the professional/salaried class's tradition of generally distrusting the monarch's intentions. This, as Samuel Huntington asserted a long time ago, meant that they inevitably saw "the monarch's reforms as too little and too late, an insincere sop designed to mask hard commitment to the preservation of the status quo."[36]

As mentioned, the methods of control used make both regimes good candidates for the denotation of (neo)patrimonial rulership. However, in characterizing these states, it would be wrong to stop here. The organization and functioning of both of these states and their relationship to economic processes and social structures were significantly different from the patrimonial rules of the past. Furthermore, the formation and maintenance of these repressive regimes were also related to demands originating on a global level.

The shah's and the Somoza family's dominance was not based on "the inner support in the subjects' compliance with the norms . . . [which] derive from tradition."[37] Rather, it was fundamentally guaranteed on the basis of economic rewards or repression. Neither of these brought real loyalty. The ideological element in their rulership (hegemony) was secondary. As James Petras and Morris Morley have pointed out, there was no sense in which authority was "freely recognized as a source of legitimacy." Instead, authority was embodied in the "fear generated by the use or threat of force."[38] It was this ever-present threat of the "stick," represented in the omnipresence of the feared Iranian SAVAK and the Nicaraguan National Guard, that made the economic rewards so hard to refuse.

Regarding global exigencies, these states were responding to economic as well as politico-strategic demands. The politico-strategic demands essentially arose from the two countries' strategic position (Iran's closeness to the Soviet Union and Nicaragua's location for a transoceanic canal) and the need to stabilize their position within the context of great power rivalry (i.e., keep them in the Western camp). The economic demands emanated from the need to create the optimal conditions for dependent capitalist development. This combination of politico-strategic and eco-

nomic demands contributed to the development of states specifically
geared toward systematic demobilization of the masses.

State, Economic Processes, and Prominent Classes

The argument I have made so far suggests that state autonomy and
personal control were dominant state features in Iran and Nicaragua. In
other words, neither state was dominated by a particular class. This was
because the capitalist classes in these countries did not have the economic
presence or political capability to shape their respective states. In Iran,
the attempts by the intermediate classes to gain control during the Mossadeq
era and the early 1960s also proved ineffectual due to the lack of internal
cohesion and external pressures. The major question here is why states
that were autonomous from the rising capitalist class ultimately opted for
an industrial policy favoring that class to the detriment of integrated
economic growth.[39]

In Iran, the immediate motivation and ideological basis for capitalist development was nationalism, spurred by more than half a century of
Western economic encroachment. This is not to say that the shah was
inspired by nationalism. Rather, his actions must be interpreted as a
reaction to the nationalist movement that swept the country in the 1950s
and demanded an end to national degradation. Once the shah survived
attacks against his regime, he found the best way to consolidate power
was to pursue capitalist development. He could not have pursued a
radical policy since his reinstatement as the supreme leader occurred
through crushing the working-class movement. The radicalization option
was also precluded by U.S. support. The pursuit of capitalist development was the best option for two reasons. First, it was made easy by the
weakness of the landed upper class. Second, it allowed the shah to gather
support, at least originally, from segments of the nationalist movement.

This state initiative in fostering capitalist development, however,
could not have been an exercise in autonomous capitalist development.
As Ellen Kay Trimberger has convincingly pointed out, capitalist development independent of foreign control was impossible even for Japan one
hundred years ago.[40] Despite the ability to generate its own capital and
prevent foreign investment, Japan's economic development was distorted
by dependence on advanced capitalist economies for heavy machinery
and raw material. The Iranian economy was also blessed with the necessary capital for industrial investment, but this capital came from the
export of oil and not from taxing the peasants in the Meiji manner. That
is, it was not dependent on mass mobilization for a vast productive effort
and the sacrifice of immediate consumer fulfillment. Neither was feasible,

given the way the shah was brought back to power, or necessary. But this meant that the problem of adequate capital formation through internal accumulation was never solved, which explains the increasing dependence on oil exports.[41]

From the 1960s onward, the Iranian economy was geared toward the state's capture and redistribution of a share of the economic surplus from oil production. The capture of surplus was accomplished through taxation, royalties, and direct claims of profits (when Iran juridically became the sole owner). The government, in turn, used the surplus for its own financial support (including military purchases and the maintenance of military personnel), the development of other economic sectors, and large public-expenditure programs (e.g., welfare programs, public-works construction, and increased state employment) to inhibit challenges to the existing political structures.

Given the low level of accumulated capital in private hands, the Iranian state was the only source of direct investment in basic industry. However, surplus distribution into other economic sectors took the form of import substitution (IS) for the newly generated internal market. Like so many other peripheral social formations, Iran used IS to encourage the establishment and growth of manufacturing firms producing goods that had been previously imported from abroad. High tariffs and import-licensing were designed to give Iranian entrepreneurs, and increasingly their foreign partners, a strong competitive edge over foreign firms producing the same goods. At the same time, the government used internal licensing to restrict the amount of internal competition with which a new producer must contend.

Originally, these policies were geared toward the production of light industrial goods for the internal market. However, increasing revenues from oil production allowed Iran to switch to export promotion and the development of heavy industry (e.g., steel, heavy-metal plants, aluminum smelters, and petrochemicals). Plans were made for exploring the world's second-largest known reserve of natural gas, mining and processing cooper, and building automotive and other machine industries and nuclear plants.

This ambitious, state-guided industrialization process initiated by the shah explains the increasing size and importance of the salaried/professional class in civil society. This class included the civil bureaucrats as well as nongovernmental members of the salaried/professional class whose technocratic and managerial abilities had become indispensable to private bureaucracies. Another aspect of the Iranian economy was that the rapid industrialization process did not lead to the doom of the traditional petty bourgeoisie. This class, which included traders, small entrepreneurs, shopkeepers, and merchants, was mostly integrated in the

centers of petty-commodity production in the urban areas—the bazaars—
and had been a part of the Iranian economy for a long time. There were,
of course, some well-to-do urban entrepreneurs with investments outside
the bazaars, but the core of this class operated within the traditional
economic structure. This class also included an estimated 90,000 clergy
who were linked to the bazaar through family and financial ties.[42] This
class was generally left out of the process of state-building and economy-
building. Yet despite this, and perhaps because of it, the members of this
class continued to rely on their wealth and to remain independent of the
state.

Abrahamian best explains the situation:

> Despite the recent growth of modern industry, the propertied middle class,
> a predominantly traditional force, had succeeded in preserving much of its
> power. The bazaars continued to control as much as half of the country's
> handicraft production, two-thirds of its retailed trade, and three-quarters
> of its wholesale trade. The bazaars retained their independent craft and
> trade guilds, whereas most all other occupations lost their unions and
> professional associations. . . . Moreover, the clergy continued to control a
> large, though decentralized, establishment. . . . In fact, the prosperous 1960s
> allowed well-to-do bazaars to finance the expansion of the major seminaries.
> Paradoxically, prosperity had helped strengthen a traditional group.[43]

In other words, like the salaried/professional class, the petty bourgeoisie
constituted an important part of the modern Iranian social structure
in the 1970s. And, again like the salaried/professional class, it maintained
a lukewarm but nevertheless supportive attitude toward the regime.

With the oil boom, however, the picture began to change. A rift
began to develop between the clique surrounding the shah, which was
publicly enriching itself with the oil money,[44] and these two prominent
classes. This was not the first time these two classes, with seemingly
contradictory interests, had joined to question the institution of monarchy.
The Constitutional Revolution of 1906–11 and the oil nationalization
movement of the early 1950s had both resulted in the reinstatement of
the institution of monarchy. Why was it different this time? Why did the
mechanisms that proved so effective in stabilizing the country ultimately
bring about the opposite results? Before laying out the answers to these
questions, a closer look at the Nicaraguan situation will also be instructive.

Although the best-known aspects of the Nicaraguan state were
personalization of power and cronyism, these should not obscure the
important role the state came to play in the economy. To be sure, the
extent of state guidance of the economy was not nearly as extensive as in
the Iranian case; however, as Carlos Vilas points out, the Nicaraguan

state belonged to the Somoza family but, in its own way, was also the state of capital.[45] As such, it greatly assisted the modernization and diversification of the economy, began in the 1950s, by constructing the infrastructure and financing. It is true most of these efforts promoted activities in which the Somoza family had a share, but they also helped entrench a particular form of capitalism.

Nicaragua's version of capitalism had its roots in its incorporation into the international division of labor as an exporter of primary products, with coffee emerging as the most important crop by the end of nineteenth century.[46] By World War II, however, coffee's dynamism as an export crop began to decline considerably. No other agricultural crop was able to match the importance of coffee in the Nicaraguan economy until cotton began to be marketed aggressively. Between 1950 and 1965, cotton's share of total Nicaraguan exports went from 5 percent to 45 percent. The Nicaraguan state promoted cotton production through road construction to expedite transport to storage, distribution centers, and ports. In addition, the government's extension of credit facilitated the cotton producer's access to agrochemical inputs, new seed varieties, and the purchase of machinery and equipment. The government also provided cheap loans and technical assistance for the promotion of other agroexports, such as tobacco, beef, shrimp, bananas, and irrigated rice—in which the Somoza family often had a share. In general, no matter where subsidized inputs went, they were directed toward large producers for export or processing activities connected to export crops.

This governmental assistance in promoting and managing the cotton boom of the 1950s explains the somewhat tenuous marriage of convenience struck between the Somoza-controlled state and economic empire and the Nicaraguan bourgeoisie that began to modernize with the expansion of cotton production. In this relationship, three centers of economic power—representing different though overlapping interest groups based on the progressive fusion of commercial and financial capital with agroindustrial and productive capital—emerged and learned to share the fruits of the cotton boom, even though not always in a smooth fashion.

First and foremost was the Somoza clan itself. It held wide holdings in practically every segment of the economy. It had its own financial networks, owned one-fifth of the nation's arable land, produced and processed such export products as cotton, sugar, coffee, cattle, and bananas, held vital import-export franchises, had extensive investment in urban real estate, and owned or had controlling interests in two seaports, a maritime line, the national airline, the concrete industry, and various other businesses.[47]

The other two economic groups centered around two financial

groups that had their roots in the power-sharing agreements of the late 1940s. The Banco de America (BANAMERICA) group was the modern expression of the traditional Conservative interests and continued to rest on old sources of economic power, like sugar and livestock. The Banco Nicaraguense (BANIC) group, which was the more important non-Somoza finance group, represented the more dynamic sector of the economy centered around cotton as well as interests linked to U.S. transnationals (e.g., Pepsi-Cola, General Mills, and United Fruit). Despite differences, all three groups coexisted peacefully until the 1970s and benefited from the state's ability to control the labor movement and to promote capitalist expansion. Black best explains the nature of their economic agreement:

> Conventionally, BANIC is described as *Banco Liberal* and BANAMERICA as the *Banco Conservador*. In practice the distinction was not so rigid. Shared economic interests, political convenience and the peculiarities of the Nicaraguan state made for considerable interpenetration as well as competition, not only between the two groups but also in partnership with Somoza. Whatever the relative strengths of BANIC and BANAMERICA, the new wealth of the post-war boom was dominated by the Somoza family.[48]

The subordinate economic position of the bourgeoisie also explains their political behavior. Lacking the ability to aspire to effective power, they generally limited themselves to pressuring the state to concede some favorable treatment in the form of credits, exports facilities, fair competition, and the like. So long as the dictatorship was willing to share, the relationship continued without serious problems.

The Somoza state's relationship to the intermediate classes was more complex. This complexity was essentially derived from the important role the intermediate classes played in Nicaragua's rural and urban class structures. In the rural areas, while large, multifamily farms had a high concentration of land (1.5 percent of these farm units controlled 41.2 percent of the land), medium-sized family and multifamily units were also important in the tenure structure (almost half the total units held more than half the land).[49] At the same time, however, family income generated by these farms was relatively low.[50] Of course, given the powerful financial groups' control over finance, trade, and processing and the state's penchant for motivating large agroexporters, the continuation of this pattern should not be surprising and can explain small and medium producers' uneasiness toward the state and large producers. This uneasiness was intensified by the fact that medium-sized producers contributed almost half of the total agricultural production.[51]

In the nonagricultural sector, the intermediate classes also had a very important presence. Nicaragua's entry into the Central American Common Market in 1963 initiated a process of urbanization that gave rise to a relatively large urban intermediate class, made up of small entrepreneurs, handicraft and petty-service undertakings,[52] employees in the bank and insurance companies, teachers, middle-rank officials in the administration and other intellectual professions, and many university-student aspirants. According to Harold Jung, this stratum, which shaded easily into the marginal bourgeoisie on the one hand and the urban working class on the other, comprised around one-fifth of Nicaragua's economically active population in 1973.[53] Like its counterpart in Iran, this class enjoyed higher educational standards than the rest of the population did, but its economic, cultural, and political aspirations were arbitrarily blocked by the regime. Given the extent of repression and economic appeasement, however, this class began to articulate its disenchantment with the Somoza regime only when it witnessed the abuses of political and economic power after the 1972 earthquake.

As many observers have pointed out, Anastasio Somoza's abuse of power when he abandoned the family tradition of relative moderation in dealing with the other important economic groups had already begun to irritate many Nicaraguans prior to the earthquake. The encroachment of his economic empire into almost all sectors of the Nicaraguan economy also had antagonized many people.[54] The ultimate abuse of power came at the disastrous Christmas earthquake of 1972, when Somoza and his associates enriched themselves shamelessly with the international aid intended for earthquake victims. The earthquake, which cost the lives of more than 10,000 people and leveled a 600-square-block area in the heart of Managua, afforded Somoza the opportunity to perform the role of a concerned and patriotic leader intending to rebuild the country. Instead, the city of Managua was rebuilt on Somoza's land by Somoza's construction companies, with international aid funneled through Somoza's banks. The extent of corruption, together with the expansion of Somoza's empire into areas of economic activity previously reserved for other members of Nicaragua's bourgeoisie, alienated large sectors of the prominent classes. Among Nicaragua's subordinate classes, the economic adversity stimulated more radical opposition, manifested in the wave of strikes, demonstrations, and land seizures that swept the country in 1972–73.[55]

As in Iran, the development of the opposition was not a new phenomenon in Nicaragua. It went back to the peasant insurrection led by Augusto Sandino in the 1920s. Yet earlier popular attempts to overthrow the regime were crushed, while the conservative bourgeois opposition was repeatedly appeased. The difference in the 1970s, as in the case of Iran, was the coincidence of internal crisis with a permissive world context that caused the prominent classes to follow a revolutionary route and rendered the state unable to stop them.

The Revolutionary Political Conjuncture

For many years, the Iranian and Nicaraguan states, personified by Mohammad Reza Pahlavi and Anastasio Somoza, dominated their respective societies through economic appeasement of potential competitors, elaborate repressive machinery, and U.S. support. In time, however, these bulwarks of support produced their opposite.

Economic Crisis and the Politics of Decline

As mentioned earlier, the Iranian and Nicaragua states were based on an opportunistic and classless form of governance. These characteristics essentially led to a situation where almost all classes and groups could be identified with either the regime or the regime's opposition. This is why both states were distinguished by attempts to gain whatever support they could get—cutting across class lines—through economic appeasement and repressive tactics directed at almost every sector of the society. This is also why any form of economic crisis was threatening to the stability of these regimes.

Interestingly, economic crisis was almost inevitable, given the types of political economy created by both regimes. Even in Iran, despite impressive economic performance,[56] the oil-based economic strategy was a mixed blessing in that it inhibited the development of a stable and developing capitalist order.[57] The reasons for this must be found in the fact that the ample flow of foreign-exchange reserves (1) reduced the urgency of promoting and expanding efficient non-oil export industries, and (2) weakened the government's resolve to implement reforms of the taxation system to guarantee a dependable source of income for the government.

The lack of efficient non-oil export industries has been extensively documented elsewhere.[58] Here, it is sufficient to note that attempts to diversify the economy did not prove very effective; non-oil exports fell from 20 percent in 1962 to about 4 percent of the exports in 1976.[59] This is important because, while Iran benefited from the quadrupling of oil prices in 1973–74, it also suffered from the reduced demand for oil in the 1975–76 recession.[60] Interestingly, but not surprisingly, although the attempt to diversify the economy was not successful, it nevertheless created a serious drain on petrodollars. In the manufacturing sector, for instance, since the local content of production was limited to assembly operation, there was an insatiable appetite for foreign intermediate and capital goods. The same drainage occurred in the agricultural sector, when much of the government investment was redirected toward large-scale, capital-intensive (including foreign agribusiness) projects in the hope of improving agricultural productivity.[61] In short, the problems in the Iranian economy were not much different from the inefficiencies and lack of intersectoral linkages encountered by other peripheral formations that have attempted industrialization through import substitution.[62] These problems were just worsened because oil revenues reduced the need for efficient production.

The lack of an efficient tax system, on the other hand, is a phenomenon distinctive to countries that have at their disposal nontax government revenues.[63] The abundant flow of foreign exchange was indeed a luxury in Iran since it took away the need to tax the traditional sector to generate surplus for the modern sector. This absence of the need to implement unpopular reforms of the taxation system would not have caused any problems had foreign exchange continued to pour into the country and had the government not overextended its social, economic, and military responsibilities. But the combination of import-intensive industrialization, heavy social and armed expenditures, and an inefficient tax system created a serious balance of payment problem.

Indeed, by 1970, the Iranian economy had a large accumulated deficit that would have required the adoption of some sort of economic stabilization program had it not been for the dramatic rise in oil prices.[64] Although the oil boom temporarily solved the deficit problem, it ultimately exaggerated the imbalances of the economy since the structure of decision making and the goals did not change. The oil boom simply meant more grandiose industrial schemes, more social spending, and a lot more arms spending. To that were added inflationary pressures, shortages of skilled manpower, acute infrastructural bottlenecks, and corruption.

It is true that between 1973 and 1975 almost every sector of the society benefited as a result of the government policy of injecting oil wealth into the economy through public expenditures. Before too long, however, this infusion created an overheated economy. With the advent of inflation, most of the immediate material benefit accruing to various classes began to disappear, while speculation in land became the main drain for accumulated capital. Economic stability, which had been the hallmark of the previous decade, was undermined. More important, governmental economic tactics, developed within the context of an economy addicted to rising oil revenues, proved inadequate in dealing with these problems, especially since the oil boom began to dissipate by 1977.

In an attempt to respond to the demands of various constituencies and to stabilize the economy, the government flip-flopped in its policies. It first attacked business interests. The policies of price control, wage increases, antiprofiteering, and share participation adversely affected the entrepreneurial bourgeoisie as well as the petty-bourgeois interests in the bazaars.[65] The outcome of these policies was increased governmental intervention in the economy without noticeable improvement in economic conditions. These policies thus served to intensify grievances against the state. By 1977, the government was ready to use a different strategy. Spearheaded by a new cabinet containing a number of industrialists, the new economic strategy was geared toward larger-business interests.[66] It called for economic liberalization in the form of relaxing price controls and antiprofiteering campaigns. This liberalization, however, was not extended to the bazaar community, which continued to face fixed prices set by the Chamber of Guilds—a governmental representative.

These contradictory policies reflected the government's inability to reconcile the interests of the entrepreneurial bourgeoisie, which were supposed to be the keystone of the economic model of development it had chosen, and the other social classes, which were becoming weary of increased prices. The only constant in government economic policy during this period was the attack on the interests of one class—the traditional petty bourgeoisie—to control inflation. This class was also subject to increased and retroactive taxation to pay for extended governmental programs. The lack of an efficient tax system to funnel capital from the traditional sector to the modern sector was now haunting the regime, whose new taxation policies led to vehement protests by the bazaar guilds against arbitrary regulations.[67] In other words, the belated post-1975 attempts to generate surplus internally threw the economy into disarray and created a rift between the traditional petty bourgeoisie and the state that ultimately proved to be very dangerous for the latter.

The economic crisis that engulfed Nicaragua in the 1970s also created a rift between the prominent classes and the state, but its dynamics were a bit different. Like other heavily export-oriented dependent economies, the Nicaraguan economy had always fluctuated with the vagaries of the international market.[68] In the 1970s, a four-year drought, combined with the decreasing value of cotton, sugar, and meat exports, created an economic convulsion not easily overcome even by the relative buoyancy of coffee prices (in 1976–77) and a false postearthquake boom (in 1973–74). Hence, after 1974, economic growth was always combined with astronomical foreign debt,[69] and investment showed negative growth (except in 1977). In 1978, GDP fell by 5 percent, and foreign debt reached $1 billion, marking a fourfold rise over six years.[70] Somoza had always been considered creditworthy, but these economic problems raised questions about his credit rating. Black explains the consequences:

> Once the Interamerican Development Bank and the World Bank began to question soft loans to Somoza, he had no alternative but to turn to assistance on harsher terms, appealing to 133 U.S. private banks. Domestic measures to ease the balance of payment crisis only weakened Somoza's political situation. In 1978 his congress introduced a bill to end tax exemption on industrial profits. The move gave the government an extra $17 million in revenue but antagonized yet another sector of the bourgeoisie.[71]

Ultimately, even the International Monetary Fund, which had continued to extend credit to the regime, grew dissatisfied. A loan request was rejected at the end of 1978, and a 1979 loan was only accepted after the imposition of austerity measures, which devalued Nicaragua's currency and instituted economic reforms. The enforced devaluation sealed the fate of Somocismo. It hit the small and medium-sized enterprises harshly, and many were driven into bankruptcy. Somoza realized the lethal effects of devaluation and attempted for one last time to salvage the remains of his regime by making wild populist promises. But even the newly decreed wage increases could not keep up with inflationary pressures. More important, the intensity of the political and economic convulsion had robbed the regime of one of its traditional means of generating political support: economic pacts with the other power contenders.

Meanwhile, the rift between the private sector and the government began to widen. In 1974, Nicaragua's principal industrial and commercial chambers, united as the Superior Council of Private Initiative (Consejo Superior de la Iniciativa Privida—COSIP), sponsored a convention of private-sector interests that demanded greater honesty in government and social reforms. According to Vilas, the demands of the private sector essentially centered around guarantees of general use of the social surplus rather than exclusive use by certain members of the capitalist clique. At the same time, the private sector clamored for participation in the management of public affairs. As such, "the kind of state demanded by the Nicaraguan bourgeoisie was a modern capitalist state that would efficiently fulfill its political-economic functions."[72]

This attempt to transform the Nicaraguan state ultimately led to the creation of the Democratic Union for Liberation (UDEL) in 1974, which united various parties and political groups situated in the middle of the political spectrum. Of course, UDEL's success against the dictatorship was at best limited. Two weeks after its formation, a guerrilla Christmas raid on a party thrown at the house of the minister of agriculture afforded Somoza the excuse to establish a state of siege, martial law, and press censorship for the next thirty-three months. These emergency measures temporarily silenced outward expression of dissatisfaction. But the continued pillage of the economy and regime brutality increased the separation between the business opposition and the dictatorship that was suffocating its democratic aspirations without giving it substantial economic benefits. One could even argue the state of siege actually gave the business opposition a point to rally around: the need to return to institutional normality. This call for democratization gained more momentum as international politics changed at the end of 1976 with the election of U.S. President Carter. Political changes in the United States actually proved pivotal for the Iranian situation as well.

The Changing World Context

As mentioned earlier, the United States had been implicated in the creation and consolidation of the Iranian and Nicaraguan regimes. This had always been a sore point for the nationalist forces in both countries, but the unwavering nature of U.S. support discouraged the opposition from attempting to alter the situation. Important shifts in global politics and economics in the 1970s, however, were instrumental in the intensification of nationalist sentiments (particularly in Iran) and the breakdown of control mechanisms.

In Iran, nationalist sentiments were intensified with increased U.S. visibility and connections, which manifested themselves in several ways. First, there was a swelling in the number of Americans working and living in Iran.[73] Second, there was a dramatic increase in trade between the two countries. This was, however, a one-sided relationship as Iran became the repository of U.S. manufactured goods (both military and nonmilitary).[74] U.S. investment in Iran also peaked. U.S. capital had never been exceedingly enthusiastic about Iran, but the oil boom was simply too appealing to resist.[75] Finally, the U.S. cultural penetration intensified during the oil boom. The infatuation with everything "American," which had prompted a prominent Iranian writer to complain about the phenomenon of "Westoxication" a decade earlier, reached new heights with the deluge of Western consumer goods, television programs, and movies.

The U.S. penetration in Iran never reached the magnitude of the infiltration of, for instance, prerevolutionary Mexico. Díaz's regime in Mexico, however, was at least born in nationalism and led by one of the heroes of the war against the French occupation, even though it came to symbolize the betrayal of the nation.[76] The shah, on the other hand, never enjoyed a nationalist reputation, and, as one observer reports, his "primary vulnerability was a consequence of a deeply held conviction among Iranians that his regime, with all its brutality and corruption, was the creation of American policy."[77] The increased reliance on Western technology and know-how, capital goods, and modern weapons merely reaffirmed his notoriety as an antinationalist leader.

The shah did attempt to portray his nationalist disposition in the early 1970s, when he became one of the main forces behind OPEC's price increases. His obsession with military buildup, however, abrogated any advances made while taking this hawkish stand on the oil prices. After a visit to the United States in November 1977, the shah was promised more arms, and the tough stand was abandoned in favor of moderation within OPEC. His linkage was simply too strong to allow any systematic opposition to U.S. interests for a prolonged period. This was especially true in the 1970s because of the increasing importance of Iran to U.S. foreign policy. The U.S. defeat in Indochina, the perceived futility of employing the strategy of direct intervention by U.S. forces, and the subsequent promulgation of the Nixon doctrine, which delegated a front-line role to local troops to guard against communist infiltration, made Iran the prime candidate for becoming the "gendarme" of the Persian Gulf. This, in conjunction with the shah's own desire to fuel his military, led to a massive military buildup that was a mixed blessing. It did increase the international prestige of the regime. It allowed, for instance, the Iranian armed forces to enter Oman in 1973 and help crush the revolutionary movement in the southern province of Dhofar. At the same time, however, the regime became even more dependent on the presence of U.S. personnel. The presumed inability of Iranians to utilize arms purchases properly gave the United States leverage over any Iranian intention running contrary to U.S. interests.[78] This meant that diplomatic pressure from the United States could put the shah's government in a bind since it was militarily dependent on the United States but politically reliant on increasingly nationalistic Iranians.

The U.S. involvement in Vietnam affected the relationship with Iran in another way. After the fall of Saigon in 1975, the United States was temporarily reluctant to engage in Third World military ventures. The so-called Vietnam syndrome had set in, making the shah's main international supporter defensive. This defensiveness led to a reevaluation of U.S. foreign policy, and, during this reevaluation, Iran was dragged into internal U.S. politics. This was a period of continual conflict between Congress and the presidency over the shape of foreign policy,[79] and the question of selling arms to a clearly authoritarian regime became a heated public issue. The repressive techniques of the shah's regime were also brought to the fore by organizations like Amnesty International and the vociferous Iranian student movement in the United States. Had the shah not been so intensely concerned about his international image, this would not have constituted any pressure on the regime. But the shah's obsession with image proved to be very debilitating to the Iranian state.

Finally, the election of Jimmy Carter in 1976 brought about a period of confusion, as the new president preached human rights while simultaneously toasting the shah as the guardian of the "island of stability." As Barry Rubin has pointed out, the Carter administration never wavered in its public support of the shah.[80] The confusion seems to have reflected the shah's own insecurities. He had always felt uncomfortable with Democratic presidents, because they reminded him of John Kennedy's imposition of a reformist prime minister in the early 1960s.[81] In reality, his concern about Carter's human rights policy was unwarranted.[82] It did point to the fact that even the shah was not free from collective paranoia about foreign control—seeing foreign conspiracies at every turn of events—which has been a strong feature of Iranian political life.[83] In the last analysis, however, it really did not matter whether there was a conspiracy or not since the shah, who was the core of the state, feared that the Democratic president might attempt to undermine his rule. As will be demonstrated later, this personal fear, which was compounded by internal factors, hinted at the first signs of state disintegration.

The U.S. relationship with Nicaragua was much less complicated. As mentioned earlier, U.S. military and economic aid to Nicaragua had been an immensely important resource for the Somoza dynasty to draw on in its successful attempt to control the Nicaraguan society. Using U.S. military support, it violently crushed lower-class uprisings, which convinced the upper and intermediate classes of the futility of any internally generated opposition. The U.S. policy of unquestioned support continued amidst the social turmoil of the mid-1970s as Anastasio Somoza, using the occasion of the guerrilla attack on a Managua Christmas party, secured an 80 percent increase in U.S. military aid to create an elite counterinsurgency force within the National Guard. This increase in aid was presumably requested to fight guerrilla forces (still fewer than a hundred) in northern Nicaragua. Instead, a campaign of terror was directed against the rural population there, and it has been reported that close to 80 percent of the rural population was uprooted into settlement camps.[84] Such gross violations of human rights appalled Nicaragua's moderates and intensified Somoza's international notoriety. When the Carter administration unveiled its human rights policy in 1977, Nicaragua became one of its principal targets. Nicaragua constituted what William LeoGrande calls a "near-perfect showcase" for the policy: "The FSLN, never a serious threat to Somoza regime, had not been heard from since their Christmas operation. The absence of any apparent security problem in Nicaragua meant that U.S. policy there, unlike toward Iran and South Korea, could be safely guided by the moral imperative of human rights undiluted by national security concerns."[85]

This quotation is not intended to suggest the Carter administration was planning to undermine an ally of U.S. foreign policy. On the contrary, the intention was to enhance U.S. international prestige without destabilizing a friendly regime. This policy ultimately proved faulty on two grounds. First, questioning Somoza's human rights record and subsequently cutting off military aid emboldened the moderate opposition, which historically had been immobilized by unquestioned U.S. support for the dynasty, and created room for the Sandinista Front of National Liberation (FSLN) to resurface and engage in its military and political operations. Second, because of Somoza's close connections to several U.S. Congresspeople, the cut in aid set off a debate in the United States that became increasingly intense as the insurrection deepened and the possibility of harm to U.S. national interests grew. The result of all this was confusion in the U.S. foreign-policy establishment, which led to further weakening of a regime whose survival had traditionally depended on solid U.S. support.[86] LeoGrande is once again instructive:

> As civil war became endemic, U.S. policy was caught in the pull of opposing imperatives. Should the United States stand by its advocacy of human rights and democratic reform in the face of Somoza's deteriorating political position? Or should human rights be subordinated to the political stability long provided by a brutal but reliable ally? Complicating this choice was the Carter Administration's self-imposed prohibition on interventionism in the Hemisphere and uncertainties as to whether Somoza could, in fact, restore order. To some extent, differing evaluations of the situation tended to be bureaucratically based. The ability of the Administration to devise a coherent policy was further diminished by the potent "Nicaragua lobby" in Congress, and its willingness to hold unrelated legislation hostage to the Administration's actions. This interplay of forces resulted in a policy which was more a product of bureaucratic compromise than a clear assessment of U.S. interests. In fact, there was hardly a policy at all.[87]

In other words, as in Iran, it was never a systematic U.S. policy to weaken the regime in Nicaragua, but the effect of most U.S. actions was the same. In both cases, when internal pressures to reform intensified, the United States did not pursue a consistent policy of solid support for the individual leaders involved. This cracked open states that by then had become mere representations of the individual leaders.

Revolutionary Conjuncture and the
Breakdown of Methods of Control

The wavering of U.S. support was clearly important in shaking the dictators in Iran and Nicaragua. But state breakdown was ultimately assured when internal methods of control failed to contain the population. In both cases, methods of control that had worked effectively for years turned out to be quite ineffective as the revolutionary crisis deepened. In fact, these methods helped to undermine the regimes even further.

In Iran, the ineffectiveness of these methods became apparent when the regime actually attempted to mobilize the social base it had been lacking. The shah created the Resurgence party and announced a one-party system in 1975. The existing two parties were merged, and membership was required of most government and university employees, as well as many others.[88]

Since the previous two-party system had been a farce, the creation of the Resurgence party simply did away with the democratic facade. But the manner in which the party was imposed antagonized what might have been a loyal opposition.[89] It confirmed once again that the shah would not even tolerate political independence on the part of high-ranking civilian leaders. The party, helped by SAVAK, attempted to penetrate various ministries, the organizations dealing with communications and mass media, the rural cooperatives, the bazaars, and the religious establishment. The attempt to penetrate the bazaars was the first such effort in Iranian history and included such tactics as opening branches within the bazaars, setting a minimum wage for workers, forcing donations from small businessmen, dissolving the traditional guilds, and creating new ones. The religious establishment was also hit hard when special investigators began to scrutinize the accounts of religious endowments and the government tried to monopolize the publication of theology books.[90]

The timing of the formation of the Resurgence party also proved to be inopportune. The announcement came just as the beneficial effects of the oil boom were fizzling and the administrative demands created by the boom were congesting the bureaucracies. This meant that the much-needed attempt to mobilize the population and create a social basis for the regime led to further centralization of an already overextended bureaucracy. The result was fear and resentment among various bureaucracies unable to respond to the innumerable problems that suddenly faced them and a general weakening of the regime. The reason for this was fairly simple. For more than a decade, the political tactics developed were intended to demobilize the population. Accordingly, the regime had never cultivated institutional mechanisms to forge links between the state and society. To sell the Resurgence party to the people, the state had to use the old institutions developed not to mobilize but to control people. The effort to mobilize thus became an elaborate exercise in mass manipulation, and as such it was deeply resented. More important, this exercise was very costly to the state apparatus because it overburdened it with additional, and very extensive, responsibilities.

Although the Resurgence party debilitated the regime, it was the core of the regime that caused its disintegration. At the core was the shah himself. Given his elevated structural role, his soundness of mind and body was pivotal for the perpetuation of the state he had erected. There were two obstacles hindering his customary decision-making capabilities during this period. The first was that he suffered from cancer. He probably realized that, on the one hand, he did not have long to live and, on the other hand, his son and heir was too young and too weak to rule effectively. It is important to mention that the Iranian monarchy, given its identification with foreign powers from its inception, was not truly endowed with an institutionalized means of succession furnished to monarchies by the mystification of royal blood.

The second was Carter's human rights policy which, as mentioned, gave the shah contradictory signals about U.S. support. The combination of these two factors left the shah with little personal incentive to continue as a dominant force. In fact, both the British and U.S. ambassadors, who had close daily contacts with him in his last months in power, report on his despondent mood and his belief that the Americans had decided to undermine his rule.[91] Hence, even before his last months, the combination of personal and foreign pressures resulted in policies that proved fatal.

After the failure of the Resurgence party to institutionalize the monarchy, the shah embarked on a policy of liberalization. It was during this period that all the tactics of political control developed during the previous decade came to haunt the regime. The emasculation of the Majles and the judiciary meant that the shah was left without means for absorbing and deflecting popular protest. His inability to make decisions could only convulse a system that enjoyed no other agency to take his place. His *divide et impera* tactic prohibited collective action on the part of his subordinates and proved fatally defective during the period of revolutionary upsurge. His method of dealing with the opposition also proved counterproductive. The strategy of alternately using cooptation and repression during the previous decade meant that few opposition leaders would risk either communicating with the shah or attempting to strike a compromise, fearing the possibility of being branded as appeased or coopted. The end result of all this was that the personal political machine, enhanced at the expense of every political institution that might have saved the system, was paralyzed.

With the failure of the policy of compromise, the only option left for the shah in dealing with the popular opposition was to resort to more force. The installation of a military government, however, was also half-hearted. While the military government undermined liberties previously granted, it did not unleash brute force against the popular forces. This confused the more loyal, hard-core officers at a time when the popular forces were making headway among the military's rank and file. By December 1978, the regime no longer had any options. It had become clear the shah had to leave the country.

The only problem at this point was to find a member of the moderate opposition who would be willing to form a government and convince the loyal officers to support the new government. The appointment of Shahpour Bakhtiar was expected to curtail revolutionary fervor. To ensure the military's loyalty to the new government, the shah had already appointed three of his close military advisors to command the armed forces. In reality, the more serious problem within the military was not the loyalty of the army leadership to Bakhtiar but its disintegration from the bottom due to family and religious influences among the rank and file.[92]

With the shah's departure, organized political forces in the capital and other cities, working through and mostly around the new government, maneuvered to define and control the governmental organs. Bakhtiar's government was doomed to failure from the beginning. The fact that he was appointed by the shah made it very difficult for the moderate opposition to support him. More important, the shah had transferred to him a state that was already well into the process of disintegration. Bakhtiar's government had to compete with the Provisional Revolutionary Government (PRG), set up by Khomeini, and other popular organs for authority over its various agencies and functions. Faced with a weak civilian leadership, a visible decline in discipline, and the moderate composition of the PRG, the military announced its neutrality in the conflict between Bakhtiar and the PRG. This left Bakhtiar with no source of support. The disintegration of the apparatus identified with the shah was now complete.

The breakdown of state apparatus in Nicaragua was also quite rapid, but it had much more violent side effects.[93] In fact, despite the volatility of the early 1970s, Nicaragua seemed far from a revolution in 1977. The state of emergency declared in the winter of 1975 seemed to have won Somoza the "social peace" he had desired. The method of terrorizing opponents into silence had divided the FSLN and paralyzed UDEL. Believing social turmoil was under control, the dictator now agreed to lift the state of emergency in exchange for U.S. military credits. As soon as the state of emergency was lifted, however, the depth of social upheavals became manifest. The FSLN renewed its military operations, and the moderate opposition began to vocalize its grievances. Through a major announcement in La Prensa, the major opposition paper, twelve well-known figures from economic, cultural, and religious life called for a democratic alternative and, significantly, included the FSLN among the suggested participants in such an alternative. According to Weber, Somoza's response was typical:

> Somoza refused to make any concessions to this renewal of opposition activity. On the contrary, he raised the stakes still higher, and on 10 January 1978, Pedro Joaquín Chamorro, La Prensa director and UDEL leader, was assassinated in Managua. By eliminating the very man who embodied the liberal solution, Somoza attempted to place the Nicaraguan bourgeoisie and the Carter administration before a dire choice: 'either Somoza or the Sandino-communists'. Once again, he had deliberately opted for catastrophic politics.[94]

Somoza actually did not have many other options. He understood very well the source of his political stamina: brute force funded and trained by U.S. military assistance. To be sure, as the rule-maker in the Nicaraguan political game, he had offered political and economic amenities to the bourgeois opposition in exchange for political docility. But these offerings were always situated within the larger threat of force. Now that his longtime accomplices, working first through UDEL and later the Frente Amplio de Oposicion (FAO), were no longer interested in allowing him to make the rules, he was intent on showing them that any thought of maintaining the game without him was an unattainable dream. In this respect, Somoza understood very well the futility of the strategy of "Somocismo without Somoza" in a system in which liberal institutions and social networks had been systematically eroded. On the other hand, the bourgeois opposition, confident of the Carter administration's support and its ability to control the popular forces, was intent on forcing a negotiated compromise on Somoza, removing him from power in accordance with the constitution.

The result was an all-out confrontation in the form of strikes and mass demonstrations, which led to the regime's debilitation but not its death. In fact, apparently convinced that no one could oust him so long as he had the support of the National Guard, Somoza set out "to drown the popular movement in blood and to persuade the liberal bourgeoisie to come to terms."[95] By this time, however, the revolutionary process was well under way and was beyond the control of any one person. It could even be argued, as Weber does, that Somoza's obstinacy merely exposed the limitations of FAO's strategy in the face of a regime that did not hesitate to use violence. Somoza's behavior showed that "an enemy bent on civil war could be vanquished only by the methods of civil war, and only an armed movement could overcome the National Guard. Unless it culminated in an insurrection, any general strike would inevitably be defeated."[96] In other words, rather than quieting the bourgeois opposition, Somoza's reaction simply discredited FAO's strategy of negotiation, under an international "commission of mediation," and opened the way for the ascent of the FSLN program of national reconstruction. The final blow to FAO's conciliatory strategy, and even its existence, came on January 19, 1979, when Somoza rejected the proposals of the commission of mediation and stated he would remain in office until the end of his "electoral mandate." From this point on, the situation became one of all-out war.

The interesting question here is why a regime founded and maintained on violence was unable to defend itself successfully through violence? After all, in contrast to what happened in Iran, brute force was unleashed on the population to no avail. The answer to this question must be found in the structure of the Nicaraguan state in general and the National Guard in particular.

As mentioned before, the National Guard was clearly an indispensable tool in the Somoza family's manipulation of the Nicaraguan political scene. Yet the Guard's internal contradictions, as Weber points out, were to be the Achilles' heel of the regime.[97] These contradictions manifested themselves in the management and organization of the Guard. In regard to management, Somoza's personal style, although effective in the short run, eroded morale and discipline in the long run:

> Personal loyalty to the director in chief usually outweighed competence in promotions and assignments. Favoritism led to the protection of corruption to the point that internal discipline suffered. Manipulation of the command structure went on constantly to foil potential conspiracies: Somoza retired entire senior officer classes at once (usually at full pay and with government jobs) to eliminate potential competitors and to make room for junior officers. Especially popular or competent officers found themselves sent abroad as military attaches or retired.[98]

Clearly, such methods hurt the Guard's corporate identity. They encouraged the creation of an organization composed mainly of individual profiteers.[99] Those who did care (especially young officers) were alienated from the leadership because of corruption and the lack of professionalism in the upper ranks.

The structure of the Guard also proved inefficient in the long run. As Weber points out, the Guard was essentially a resident gendarmerie in the localities in which it was stationed. This provincial character made the Guard an effective instrument of repression, intimidation, and intelligence-gathering at the local level. It also created a profitable situation for its members, allowing them to become integrated in the local networks of corruption. But once the national insurgency gained steam, the Guard proved "incapable of military action as a national army, lacking any of the necessary training, mobility, and armour."[100] The end result was an extremely violent (given the Guard's proximity to the localities) but futile effort to sustain the Nicaraguan state. Of course, the Guard's ineffectiveness was in relation to a very impressive organized opposition. How this opposition was able to coalesce around the common goal of deposing Somoza and creating an alternative sociopolitical system is addressed in the next chapter.

Summing Up

I argued that on a very general level it was the structure of the states in Iran and Nicaragua that ultimately made them vulnerable to a cohesive, multiclass attack. I also argued that the methods of control developed to sustain these personalist regimes proved to be counterproductive during the period of revolutionary crisis. Accordingly, a particular type of state, caught in the cross fire between nationalist sentiments and external dependence and situated in a permissive world context, was singled out as distinctively susceptible to revolution. To be sure, during their successful years, these regimes did gain the backing of prominent economic classes as their state-guided industrialization policies improved the socioeconomic conditions of these classes. Yet, due to their institutional makeup and their special relationships to foreign powers, they were never able to attain the loyalty of these classes. It was the pressures exerted by these classes to bring about institutional reforms and reduce foreign influence that ultimately cracked these states open.

It is important not to overstate the rift between the prominent classes and the Iranian and Nicaraguan states. Both of these states were remarkably successful in keeping the prominent classes in check for long periods of time. These classes were not avid supporters, but they were quite happy to reap the economic benefits accrued to them and remain silent over political issues. In the 1970s, however, conflicting pressures emanating from the domestic and international environments began to intensify, causing a divergence of economic interests between the small cliques running these states and the intermediate classes. It was at this point that the intermediate classes began to compete for political power.

It is also important not to overstate the similarities between the Iranian and Nicaraguan states. For instance, they operated in different political economies. Oil-based industrialization afforded the Iranian state more room to maneuver in relation to all classes. The Nicaraguan state, on the other hand, did not have access to such a huge source of wealth. More important, situated in an agroexporting country, it was not in control of the means of production; hence, it had to negotiate with the agroexporting classes. Once these classes withdrew their support, the regime lost its balance.

Another difference can be found in the structures of the Iranian and Nicaraguan states. Although both states were dominated by one person, the Iranian state more readily heeded the bureaucratic norms, and its military was more professional. Somoza's state, with few exceptions, was essentially composed of individual profiteers. Violence and greed were part of normal politics rather than exceptions. This is an important difference and can explain the intensity of violence that was unleashed on the Nicaraguans by the National Guard. After all, by the end, it was an all-out confrontation between the National Guard, striving to survive, and the rest of the population. The role of the Iranian military was more ambiguous as the military itself began to be divided over the use of violence and defections of lower ranks became common.

As will be shown in chapter 5, the differences in the economic, class, and state structures can explain important variations in revolutionary outcomes. For instance, they can explain why the National Guard was completely disbanded while the Iranian military was essentially left in tact or why the agroexporting bourgeoisie was such an important part of the immediate postrevolutionary situation. In the next chapter, attention is turned to the societal context and the pattern of urban mobilization for a fuller understanding of the revolutionary process.

NOTES

1. The traditional Iranian state had been based on an absolutist power in which the shahs wielded supreme political authority and possessed the means of production—land. The absolutist state structure began to disintegrate under the Qajar dynasty (1796–1925) due to internal and external pressures.

2. E. Abrahamian, *Iran: Between Two Revolutions* (Princeton, N.J.: Princeton University Press, 1982), p. 149.

3. The structure of private ownership in Iran was traditionally character-

PERIPHERAL STATE, PROMINENT CLASSES, AND REVOLUTION   57

ized by the existence of state communal property and the absence of legal private property. Lands were assigned to individuals, usually members of royal households and state functionaries. These land assignments (*tuyul*) did not carry any contractual security of title to ownership, and they were temporary. This system was abolished by the first parliament (Majles) after the Constitutional Revolution at the turn of the century. This led to the creation of the legal basis of private property. For a detailed account of the system of landholding, see A. K. S. Lambton, *Landlord and Peasant in Persia* (London: Oxford University Press, 1953).

4. Abrahamian, *Iran*, pp. 340–41.

5. Constitutionalism and nationalism had been the causes of political agitation since the end of the nineteenth century. They were the demands in the Constitutional Revolution of 1906–11. The constant meddling of foreigners (especially Tzarist Russia and Great Britain) in the affairs of Iran, the increasing penetration of capitalism, and the various monarchs' inability to respond to these interventions made these two causes historically inevitable. For an excellent analysis of intervention by foreign governments, see F. Kazemzadeh, *Britain and Russia in Iran: 1864–1914* (New Haven, Conn.: Yale University Press, 1968). A good succinct history of the encroachment of capitalism can be found in N. R. Keddie, "The Economic History of Iran, 1800–1914, and Its Political Impact: An Overview," *Iranian Studies* 5 (Spring-Summer 1972), pp. 58–78.

6. F. Halliday, *Iran: Dictatorship and Development* (New York: Penguin, 1979), p. 25.

7. The most important consequence of the nationalization negotiated by the shah was that the British monopoly over Iranian oil was broken. A new consortium was established in which American, Dutch, and French capital also had shares. The nationalization also created the National Iranian Oil Company (NIOC). Effective control over price and output, however, lay with the international consortium. The NIOC was merely given a small share in production by taking over the "non-basic operations (servicing) and it also became the sole distributor inside Iran." Ibid., p. 142.

8. The CIA's involvement in the coup has been chronicled by Kermit Roosevelt, who planned the coup. See K. Roosevelt, *Countercoup: The Struggles for the Control of Iran* (New York: McGraw-Hill, 1980). For an academic analysis of the events, see B. Rubin, *Paved with Good Intentions: The American Experience in Iran* (New York: Oxford University Press, 1980).

9. H. Ladjevardi, "The Origins of U.S. Support for an Autocratic Iran," *International Journal of Middle East Studies* 15, 2 (1983), pp. 225–39.

10. Social unrest spread in the early 1960s, after the promulgation of the White Revolution. This social reform package, which included land reform, extension of suffrage to women, and expansion of social services and education, angered the bazaari merchants and the religious community, who interpreted it as yet another attempt by the state to regulate private enterprise, commerce, and religious activities. They reacted vehemently through street demonstrations. The regime reacted with force. Many of the senior ulama were arrested, and a consequential future leader—Ayatollah Khomeini—was exiled.

11. Nicaragua is the only country in Latin America other than the Dominican Republic and Cuba that has been under the direct rule of the United States.

12. J. A. Booth, "The Revolution in Nicaragua: Through a Frontier of History," in *Revolution and Counterrevolution in Central America and the Caribbean*, ed. D. E. Schultz and D. H. Graham (Boulder, Colo.: Westview Press, 1984), pp. 301–30.

13. Conflict between these two cities centered on which city should become the political capital of the country as well as significant differences in economic interests. The wealth of the self-styled aristocratic landowners of Granada was largely based on cattle and trade with the Caribbean. The small landowners and artisans of Leon, on the other hand, geared their international trade almost entirely toward the Pacific.

14. For instance, in what must be one of the most bizarre incidences in Central American history, a North American by the name of William Walker was brought into Nicaragua to aid the Liberal cause. Walker ruled Nicaragua from 1855 to 1857, with U.S. recognition. His personal control was ultimately checked by joint Central American resistance, but the Liberals' connection with this embarrassing episode opened the way for more than thirty-five years of uninterrupted rule by the Conservatives.

15. Of course, had the local elite been more cohesive and their power more institutionalized, intervention would have been less necessary to maintain U.S. strategic and economic interests.

16. See G. Selser, *Sandino* (New York: Monthly Review Press, 1981), pp. 11–20.

17. J. M. Paige, "Cotton and Revolution in Nicaragua," in *States versus Markets in the World System*, ed. P. Evans, D. Rueschemeyer, and E. H. Stephens (Beverly Hills, Calif.: Sage, 1985), p. 94.

18. Ibid., p. 109.

19. Anastasio Somoza García's ascent to power was complete by 1936, when he finally became the president of Nicaragua as the head of the Liberal party. In 1948 and 1950, he managed to get the Conservatives and Liberals to sign pacts offering the Conservatives one-third of the seats in Congress and formal guarantees of free commercial activity. These pacts gave the appearance of a two-party state (with a built-in Liberal majority) based on political representation. A similar pattern of coopting the opposition continued under the leaderships of his two sons: Luis and Anastasio.

20. G. Black, *Triumph of the People: The Sandinista Revolution in Nicaragua* (London: Zed Press, 1981), pp. 48–49. Black actually chronicles a number of episodes in U.S.-Nicaraguan collaboration, including the Bay of Pigs invasion.

21. L. Schoultz, *Human Rights and United States Policy toward Latin America* (Princeton, N.J.: Princeton University Press, 1981), pp. 58–64.

22. Between 1967 and 1975, Nicaragua, on average, received $1.8 million worth of military aid per year. Economic assistance averaged $17.3 million

annually for the same period. See J. A. Booth, *The End and the Beginning: The Nicaraguan Revolution* (Boulder, Colo.: Westview Press, 1982), p. 75.

23. See A. Perlmutter, *Modern Authoritarianism: A Comparative Institutional Analysis* (New Haven, Conn.: Yale University Press, 1981); T. Skocpol, "Rentier State and Shi'a Islam in the Iranian Revolution," *Theory and Society* 11 (May 1982), pp. 265–304; and J. A. Goldstone, "Revolutions and Superpowers," in *Superpowers and Revolution*, ed. J. R. Adelman (New York: Praeger, 1986), pp. 38–48. Goldstone's analysis is particularly good at laying out, in a succinct fashion, the vulnerabilities of neopatrimonial states.

24. For an elaborate discussion of the shah's method of governance, see M. Zonis, *The Political Elite of Iran* (Princeton, N.J.: Princeton University Press, 1971), pp. 80–117.

25. Ibid., p. 101.

26. See ibid., and Halliday, *Iran*.

27. R. Graham, *The Illusion of Power* (New York: St. Martin's Press, 1980), pp. 182–84.

28. H. Weber, *Nicaragua: The Sandinist Revolution* (London: New Left Books, 1981), p. 31.

29. T. W. Walker, "The Sandinist Victory in Nicaragua," *Current History* 78 (February 1980), p. 57.

30. Black, *Triumph of the People*, pp. 50–51.

31. Ibid., p. 52.

32. Weber, *Nicaragua*, p. 31.

33. This figure includes school teachers and health-care personnel, who elsewhere are usually reported separately. See L. S. Graham, "The Impact of the Revolution on the State Apparatus," in *Nicaragua: Profiles of the Revolutionary Public Sector*, ed. M. E. Conroy (Boulder, Colo.: Westview Press, 1987), pp. 17–39.

34. The state bureaucracy grew from twelve ministries in 1963 to nineteen ministries in 1977. During the same period, its size more than doubled, from 150,000 to 304,000 civil servants. See Abrahamian, *Iran*, p. 438.

35. Ibid., p. 432.

36. S. P. Huntington, *Political Order in Changing Societies* (New Haven, Conn.: Yale University Press, 1968), p. 163.

37. Max Weber, *Economy and Society*, 3 vols. (New York: Bedminster Press, 1968), p. 1007.

38. J. F. Petras, with M. H. Morley, P. DeWitt, and A. E. Harens, *Class, State and Power in the Third World* (London: Zed Press, 1981), p. 47.

39. This question is carefully worded to pose the problematic in a non-functionalist manner. That is, my attempt is to move away from arguments that try to explain the class content of the state by deciphering which classes benefited from state policies. The fact that the Iranian and Nicaraguan states promoted industrialization policies that benefited industrial and financial bourgeoisies does not mean that these states were necessarily dominated by them.

40. Trimberger's discussion is related to the possibility of "revolution from above." According to her, this is a specific type of revolutionary process undertaken by military bureaucrats to destroy the economic and political base of the aristocracy or upper class. E. K. Trimberger, *Revolutions from Above: Military Bureaucrats in Japan, Turkey, Egypt and Peru* (New Brunswick, N.J.: Transaction Books, 1978). The shah's "White Revolution" has been described by Bashiriyeh, and of course the shah himself, as an attempt to replicate the Bismarckian revolution from above to accelerate commodity production, transform the land-owners into a rentier bourgeoisie, construct the supremacy of generalized commerce, and lay the foundation of industrial production. Even if this were the case, it still was a shoddy attempt at best since, as will become obvious, it simply reconstructed the previous pattern of dependence. See H. Bashiriyeh, *State and Revolution in Iran, 1962–1982* (New York: St. Martin's Press, 1984).

41. In the Fifth Plan (1973–77), the oil and gas sector's share of total government revenues was about 78 percent, while the sector's share of total foreign-exchange receipts was around 85 percent. See T. Walton, "Economic Development and Revolutionary Upheavals in Iran," *Cambridge Journal of Economics* 4, 3 (1980), pp. 271–92.

42. Abrahamian, *Iran*, p. 433.

43. Ibid.

44. The figures on the amount of assets directly controlled by the shah and his close associates are not very clear. But for a discussion of how the Pahlavi economic empire operated and a partial list of economic activities, see Graham, *The Illusion of Power*, chapter 9.

45. C. M. Vilas, *The Sandinista Revolution* (New York: Monthly Review Press, 1986), pp. 83–89.

46. Coffee production reached its peak between 1920 and 1940. It came to represent between one-half to two-thirds of exports.

47. T. W. Walker, *Nicaragua: The Land of Sandino* (Boulder, Colo.: Westview Press, 1981), p. 58.

48. Black, *Triumph of the People*, p. 38.

49. Vilas, *The Sandinista Revolution*, pp. 69–71. Vilas considers a family farm as one that is "exploited without turning to the employment of a labor force outside the family of the producer—who also live on the land" (p. 275, n. 9). He also uses employment of up to twelve people and the family's participation in agricultural work as means to distinguish between medium-sized and a large, multifamily farm. The figures reported by Vilas indicate that large, multifamily farms in Nicaragua (and Costa Rica) constituted the greatest concentration of land in Central America, but they also indicate that in Nicaragua medium-sized family and multifamily farms had the highest weight in the tenure structure.

50. Ibid. Vilas's comparison to other Central American countries is quite revealing. Family income generated by these farms was $2,248 annually in Nicaragua, $8,000 in Guatemala, and something like $7,100 in El Salvador.

51. In contrast, the large agrarian bourgeoisie represented only a third of

rural population, with decisive participation only in sugarcane and rice. Of course, small and medium-sized farms were more dominant in the production for the internal market, while the large owners controlled production for the world market. Ibid.

52. Vilas reports that 54 percent of the industrial establishment employed less than five people each and could be characterized as artisanal. Ibid., p. 71.

53. H. Jung, "Behind the Nicaraguan Revolution," *New Left Review*, no. 117 (1979), p. 72.

54. Reportedly, at the end of his tenure of office, Somoza controlled an economic empire estimated to be worth nearly a billion dollars, including some 25 percent of the Nicaraguan GNP. This is an approximate figure derived from the change in the public control of economy in 1978 (15 percent) to 1980 (41 percent). According to Vilas, given that by 1980 the Area of People's Property "consisted fundamentally of the properties confiscated from the Somoza family and its allies, the difference between 1978 and 1980 gives a good approximation of the magnitude of control by the regime over the national economy." Vilas, *The Sandinista Revolution*, pp. 88–89. In any case, according to another observer, "so complete was his economic control that foreign investors avoided Nicaragua for want of any reasonable investment opportunities." See W. M. LeoGrande, "The Revolution in Nicaragua: Another Cuba?" *Foreign Affairs* 58, 1 (1979), p. 29.

55. A more detailed analysis of the activities of the subordinate classes as well as their political expression, the FSLN, will be given in the next chapter.

56. Between 1963 and 1973, Iran reported an average annual GNP growth rate of around 8 to 9 percent and a GNP per capital growth rate of 5 to 6 percent. This growth was not even throughout the economy. Manufacturing, non-oil mining, and construction grew at an average annual rate of 10 to 11 percent and services at 8 to 9 percent. During the same period, agricultural growth averaged only 2 to 3 percent. The post-1973 oil boom not only led to much higher (short-term) growth rates but also magnified the above unevenness. Services and construction jumped astronomically, while agriculture remained on the fringes. H. Katouzian, *The Political Economy of Modern Iran: Despotism and Pseudo-Modernism* (New York: New York University Press, 1981), p. 256.

57. Note that the promotion of a stable capitalist order does not entail equitable or just policies. The fact that Iran's income distribution deteriorated thus does not signify a failure of the development policy that ultimately brought out the revolutionary fervor.

58. See Halliday, *Iran*; Walton, "Economic Development and Revolutionary Upheavals"; M. Parvin and A. N. Zamani, "Political Economy of Growth and Destruction: A Statistical Interpretation of the Iranian Case," *Iranian Studies* 12 (Winter-Spring 1979), pp. 43–78; and M. H. Pesaran, "The System of Dependent Capitalism in Pre- and Post-Revolutionary Iran," *International Journal of Middle East Studies* 14, 4 (1982), pp. 501–22.

59. Parvin and Zamani, "Political Economy," p. 66–67.

60. The increase of prices in 1973–74 led to the immediate doubling of most targets of the 1973–78 Fifth Five-year Plan, and Iran became the immediate

paradise for international investment. Shortly after, however, the regime was forced to delay or completely withdraw major projects for lack of funds.

61. Despite all the investment, agricultural productivity increases (2 to 3 percent annually) continued to lag behind population increases (3 percent) and the increasing demand generated by the petrodollars. The government was increasingly forced to import food and sell it at heavily subsidized prices.

62. For a concise summary of these problems, see W. Baer, "Import Substitution and Industrialization in Latin America: Experience and Interpretations," *Latin American Research Review* 7, 1 (1972), pp. 95–122.

63. In the Iranian case, there was a decline of the share of taxes in government revenues from 32.9 percent in 1972 to 11 percent in 1974. See Bashiriyeh, *State and Revolution in Iran*, p. 98.

64. Walton, "Economic Development and Revolutionary Upheavals," p. 284.

65. Bashiriyeh, *State and Revolution in Iran*, chapter 4.

66. The turn toward the business interest was logical by this time. Although the shah's economic policies were not motivated by larger-business interests, the economic model pursued invariably gave preference to this new bourgeoisie (financial and industrial). The increasing identification with this social group — totaling no more than one thousand individuals and including members of the royal family, former larger landlords, senior civil servants, and military officers as well as old and new entrepreneurs — made it progressively difficult for the shah to reconcile their interests and ambitions with those of other social groupings. On the makeup of the new bourgeoisie, see Abrahamian, *Iran*, p. 432.

67. Bashiriyeh, *State and Revolution in Iran*, p. 103.

68. In 1977, exports accounted for 32 percent of Nicaragua's GDP. Cotton, coffee, sugar, and meat accounted for 60 percent of export earnings. See Black, *Triumph of the People*, p. 67.

69. By 1979, external debt servicing had grown to 22 percent of the value of Nicaraguan exports. Ibid.

70. Ibid.

71. Ibid.

72. Vilas, *The Sandinista Revolution*, p. 132.

73. In 1978, generally believed to be the apogee of U.S. involvement, this number reached 50,000. See K. Fatemi, "Iranian Revolution: Its Impact on Economic Relations with the U.S.," *International Journal of Middle East Studies* 12, 3 (1980), pp. 303–17.

74. In 1978, the military purchase/commitments from U.S. manufacturers amounted to over $12 billion. At the same time, the United States became the second largest supplier of Iran's nonmilitary imports, totaling $12.7 billion. Ibid.

75. For instance, at the time of the revolution, it was estimated that twelve major U.S. banks had a total capital exposure of $2.2 billion in Iran. Ibid., p. 310.

76. W. L. Goldfrank, "World System, State Structure, and the Onset of the Mexican Revolution," *Politics and Society* 5, 4 (1979), pp. 97–134.

77. R. Cottam, "American Policy and the Iranian Crisis," *Iranian Studies* 13, 1–4 (1980), pp. 301–2.

78. The question of Iran's dependence on U.S. personnel was actually debated in the U.S. Senate. The fact that this gave leverage to the United States was also discussed in a positive light. See M. Zavareei, "Dependent Capitalist Development in Iran and the Mass Uprising of 1979," *Research in Political Economy* 5 (1982), pp. 170–74.

79. F. Halliday, *The Making of the Second Cold War* (London: Verso, 1983).

80. Rubin, *Paved with Good Intentions*, chapters 7–9.

81. M. Heikal, *Iran: The Untold Story* (New York: Pantheon, 1983).

82. Rubin reports that the Carter administration directed its human rights efforts primarily against practices in the prisons and maintained public support throughout the revolutionary crisis period. Rubin, *Paved with Good Intentions*, pp. 200–201, 206, 214–15, 223, 224–25.

83. This feature has been noted by many observers of Iranian politics. It is certainly a reflection of the preponderance of foreign influence in Iranian history. For recent mention of this tendency, see S. A. Arjomand, *The Turban for the Crown: The Islamic Revolution in Iran* (New York: Oxford University Press, 1988), p. 3.

84. LeoGrande, "The Revolution in Nicaragua," p. 31.

85. Ibid.

86. Some of this confusion was reflected in the record of U.S. aid to Nicaragua during the Carter administration. In April 1977, the United States restricted both military and economic aid on human rights grounds; in September, the restrictions were relaxed. New restrictions were imposed after the assassination of an important moderate opposition leader, Pedro Joaquín Chamorro, in January 1978. Six months later, Carter sent Somoza a letter congratulating him for his improved human rights record. For a recent analysis of conflicts and confusion in U.S. foreign policy, see A. Lake, *Somoza Falling* (Boston: Houghton Mifflin, 1989).

87. LeoGrande, "The Revolution in Nicaragua," p. 33.

88. N. R. Keddie, *Roots of Revolution: An Interpretive History of Modern Iran* (New Haven, Conn.: Yale University Press, 1981), p. 179.

89. In the announcement that created the Resurgence party, the shah branded those reluctant to join the party as "Tudeh sympathizers." He also gave them the option of going to prison or leaving the country. Abrahamian, *Iran*, p. 440.

90. Ibid., pp. 440–46.

91. W. L. Sullivan, *Mission to Iran* (New York: W. W. Norton, 1981); A. Parsons, *The Pride and the Fall: Iran 1974–1979* (London: Jonathan Cape, 1984).

92. M. Sreedhar, "The Role of Armed Forces in the Iranian Revolution," *IDSA* [Institute for Defense Studies and Analysis] *Journal* 12, 2 (1979), pp. 121–42.

93. The violent nature of the Nicaraguan Revolution was reflected in the

thousands of people dead (between 20,000 to 50,000), several hundred thousands maimed or wounded, a quarter of the country's population homeless, and heavy damage to the economy, including the bombing destruction of a good part of Managua's modern industrial district. Considering Nicaragua's small population at the time of revolution (less than 3 million), these are astounding figures. The comparison to Iran, where the estimated number of persons killed was around 3,000 (out of a population of around 40 million), is also revealing. On the casualty figures in Nicaragua, see Booth, *The End and the Beginning*, p. 181. On Iran, see A. Ashraf and A. Bannuazizi, "State and Class in the Iranian Revolution," *State, Economy and Culture* 1, 3 (1985), p. 22.

94. Weber, *Nicaragua*, pp. 40–41.

95. Ibid., p. 44.

96. Ibid., p. 45.

97. Ibid., p. 32.

98. Booth, *The End and the Beginning*, p. 92.

99. Individual allegiances of the Guard were so extreme that after the 1972 earthquake the Guard dissolved. According to Booth, "Most soldiers abandoned their posts to attend their families and belongings. Somoza could not rally even a company for two days, so the U.S. and other CONDEC (Central American Defense Command) forces came to keep order." Ibid, p. 93.

100. Weber, *Nicaragua*, p. 32.

3

Urbanization and Political Protest

People generally turn to familiar routines and innovate within
them, even when in principle some unfamiliar form of action
would serve their interests much better.
— Charles Tilly,
The Contentious French

The Iranian and Nicaraguan revolutions, I have argued, were launched
by crises centered in the structure and situation of the Pahlavi and
Somoza states. Still, the actual occurrence of these revolutions depended
on how susceptible the sociopolitical structure was to sustained efforts by
popular forces to wear down the prerevolutionary regimes. These efforts
were also responsible for opening the way for revolutionary leaders to
consolidate power on the basis of more centralized and mass-incorporating
state organizations. As such, they created decisive constraints on the
range of sociopolitical options available to revolutionary leaders competing for national power. Attention is therefore turned to the particular
structural situation that facilitated the actualization of grievances against
the prerevolutionary regimes. The effect of popular revolts on the course
of national politics will be addressed in chapter 5.

As mentioned in chapter 1, the most distinguishing feature of political
mobilization in Iran and Nicaragua was that oppositional activities were
generally centered in towns and cities. Prior to these urban upheavals, both
societies experienced intense urbanization. Urbanization, however, cannot
be considered the causal factor for urban upheavals. Almost all peripheral
cities have experienced a massive infusion of people, but urban-based
revolutions are rare phenomena. In fact, recent in-depth studies have
rejected the notion that radicalism automatically accompanies migration
to the cities.[1] Where revolutions have occurred, however, the urban context invariably does affect revolutionary processes. The question is, how?

This is not an easy question to answer in the abstract. Iran and Nicaragua were very different social formations, and in the following pages I show in detail how these differences affected their differing patterns of urban mobilization. Their experience with rapid urbanization, however, produced a set of conditions that gave rise to similar social grievances. As I mentioned in chapter 1, the existence of social grievances is not unique to urban areas, but how they are directed toward the state, which is the manager of the means of daily life in the cities, makes revolutionary dynamics quite different. Unlike rural conflicts, urban antagonisms do not take the form of class conflict (between surplus producers and surplus extractors). Rather, they become conflicts between urban classes and the state, which has acquired tremendous power within the urban context. This creates the potential for the creation of a multiclass, negative coalition that can be mobilized to transform the state.

Is this potential sufficient to create revolutionary conditions? Clearly, the answer is no. I have already mentioned that the weakening of the state is a necessary condition for launching a revolution. Naturally, this weakening loosens the state's hold over civil society and creates room for the oppositional groups. But the existence of a space for oppositional activities does not necessarily lead to mobilization. Oppositional groups need to have the means to wear down the weakened state. As Charles Tilly and other students of collective action have repeatedly pointed out, a revolutionary situation is actualized when challenging groups control sufficient resources to contest effectively the sovereignty of the state.[2] To claim control over these resources, the challenging groups draw from the structures and situations afforded to them within the urban context. Since the urban classes are situated differently in relation to the state, their resources are also drawn from different sources and economic realities in the urban areas.

The professional intermediate class and skilled and semiskilled workers, as Josef Gugler points out, have an especially powerful role in the urban economy:

> Managers, professionals, skilled workers, and even semi-skilled workers in great numbers cannot be replaced at short notice. To imprison them for any length of time, to push them into exile, or to kill them entails severe economic losses. This means not only a reduction in the resources available to the state but also a deterioration in living conditions for the population at large that may foster discontent. Rather than using the stick, governments usually deal with the elements of the labor force that control key sectors of the economy such as mining, heavy industry, and transport by offering them privileges of income, fringe benefits, job security, and social security.[3]

These groups not only are "appeased" financially but also are controlled through a variety of clientelist links with state bureaucracies. But with the weakening of the state and its clientelist relationships, these classes, which objectively control key economic sectors, can use their power to shut down the urban economy and demand concessions from the government.

Another social grouping that can become politically powerful within the urban context is students. Student struggle in peripheral formations takes place primarily in the cities, where the majority of high schools and universities are located. Schools and universities constitute the point of encounter among many people who otherwise would have no common meeting ground because of the individual character of their work. As such, they offer a social space within which the isolation created by the increasing differentiation of work can be overcome, at least temporarily. In addition, schools and universities offer an arena within which students can become empowered. As the future economy-builders, students become aware that they have resources similar to the professional intermediate class and skilled workers. Furthermore, the acquired ability to articulate ideas can lead to the expression of revolutionary desires, which along with their youth—as we will see especially in the case of Nicaragua—can make students powerful organizers.

The urban poor, unlike the above social groupings, do not have much potential economic power. Their mobilization, however, adds the fire necessary to undermine the state completely. In Nicaragua, the intensity and timing of insurrection in the barrio of Monimbo even took the revolutionary leadership by surprise. Later, neighborhood organizations were transformed by external organizations like the FSLN to attack the dictatorship directly. In Iran, socioreligious bonds that existed within the poor urban communities became an indispensable resource for the religious leadership to mobilize people. In both cases, the structure of these urban communities and the links they had with external organizations connected to other social groupings allowed the urban poor to bring into the revolutionary arena political resources necessary for the overthrow of prerevolutionary regimes. This is why, to understand the pattern of mobilization, we need to look closely at how these urban communities were historically constituted and the types of linkages existing within them and with the outside world.

In general, the contribution of urban communities to the revolutionary process as "communities" (as opposed to, for instance, their class-based mobilization) is enhanced if relationships among the members are closely knit, largely autonomous from outside intervention, and based on a shared belief and value system.[4] This is why many observers have singled out traditional communities as an important organizational foundation for radical mobilization.[5] Presumably, given the existence of long-standing communal relations, such communities are more easily disturbed by any sort of intrusion, will find it easier to identify collective enemies (generally outsiders), and are more easily mobilized outside the purview of the intended targets of collective action.[6] However, such characteristics are bound to be less prominent within urban enclaves because urbanization disrupts the process through which shared understandings are reproduced. The transformation of the poor migrants into factory workers, irregularly employed workers, city-dwellers engaged in petty trade, or unemployed invariably affects the way these people relate to each other. As will be shown, this process done under strict state control does not totally prohibit the mobilization of urban communities. It does, however, limit the possibility that these communities will mobilize spontaneously and autonomously from outside organizations.

Urban Life and Revolution in Iran

Historically, urban centers in Iran have served as the focal points for demonstrations, riots, strikes, and other antiregime activities.[7] Their role became even more crucial as large groups of villagers began to move into the Iranian principal cities. Eric Hooglund, in his careful study of agricultural change after the land reform, reports that virtually every town experienced significant rural migration during the 1970s; the majority grew at average annual rates of 4 to 6 percent during the decade, in contrast to a yearly growth of less than 1 percent for the total rural population.[8]

Almost all observers of rural Iran agree that the intensity of rural migration was caused by the land reform.[9] Hooglund best describes the situation:

> The overall effect of the government's various agricultural policies was to increase the difficulties most peasants experienced in trying to make a livelihood from their landholdings. In the first place, land distribution itself did not materially benefit the majority of peasants in the sense that they acquired ownership only to plots of (at best) subsistence size. In addition, nearly half of the rural population—the agricultural laborers—had obtained no land at all. Thus, by 1971, when land reform was declared officially completed, the overwhelming majority of villagers were in no better economic situation than they had been prior to implementation of the program. Indeed the evidence suggests that the relative economic position of thou-

sands of rural families actually worsened during the "revolutionary" decade of land reform[10]

Even after the end of land reform, the flight to the cities continued as the move to capital-intensive agribusiness farming of large estates (like those in Khuzistan) in the mid-1970s further displaced thousands of day laborers.[11] In short, the situation of growing destitution in the countryside became the classic "push" factor to the cities. The thriving urban sector added a "pull" factor. There were several types of jobs available to unskilled rural migrants. The growing, labor-intensive construction industry attracted a large number of rural migrants.[12] These workers were hired on a daily basis for a given project. Manufacturing was another source of employment, although most of the manufacturing firms employing rural migrants were small scale.[13] By the mid-1970s, enterprises employing less than ten persons still accounted for more than 90 percent of all manufacturing concerns and employed 72 percent of all workers in manufacturing.[14] The jobs in larger and more prestigious enterprises were mostly reserved for skilled workers with urban origins. Finally, villagers also found employment in a wide variety of urban petty services, as domestic servants, load carriers, petty vendors, and the like. They generally lived in poor but nonsquatting urban communities.[15]

Although some migrants were absorbed into the growing urban economy, many barely survived on the fringes. This underclass dwelt in the sprawling new slums and squatter settlements, which were in sharp contrast to the luxury high-rise buildings, banks, office blocks, and exclusive residential neighborhoods where foreigners and wealthy Iranians lived. Rather than benefiting from the construction boom, many survived mostly as beggars, hoodlums, and prostitutes. Naturally, this group of impoverished immigrants had lower levels of income and occupational attainment than the nonsquatting urban poor and especially the modern industrial workers.[16] The latter social grouping, which included oil, gas, electrical, fishery, lumberyard, and transport workers as well as miners, dockers, truck drivers, and factory workers in plants of more than ten employees, constituted the most privileged grouping among the subordinate classes.[17]

Levels of income and occupational attainment were not the only differences among these subordinate social groupings. The new migrants had different prior experiences and understandings. They also differed in their relationships to the state and the intermediate classes. The migrant poor lived with their relatives in extensive and heterogeneous communities, reflecting the vastness of the country and its social diversity.[18] A vital feature of these communities was a pattern of mutual assistance, arising from the need to survive economically. Farhad Kazemi reports the existence of "networks of reciprocal exchange" with fluctuating membership.[19] He also reports that these networks never developed into secondary or voluntary associations because of tight governmental control and that "absence of sustained and effective leadership among the urban poor was a common and readily noticeable phenomenon in the 1970s."[20]

The only exception to this general pattern was the attendant activities of religious associations in squatter settlements and nonsquatting communities:

> These associations, referred to as *hay'ats*, are often organized on the basis of common ethnic or geographical origin of the members and promote religious observance and celebrate major Shi'i festivals. . . . On other occasions, the *hay'ats* in the migrant poor areas meet on a semi-regular or irregular basis in various homes of the poor and discuss common religious issues and concerns. . . . The local *hay'ats* of one migrant poor area usually have horizontal connections to other *hay'ats* in different parts of the city. They do, therefore, function loosely as networks of interrelated associations organized ostensibly for religious purposes.[21]

What was important about these religious associations was that they were forms of *external* support capable of permeating these communities because of the strong affinity of the poor with the traditional beliefs and patterns of Shi'i Islam. In addition, these bonds were constantly reinforced, since many of the regularly employed members of these communities were employed in the bazaars. As mentioned previously, the bazaars continued to be important economic centers and provided employment for many of the rural migrants. The religious establishment, which continued to adjudicate commercial disputes and provide religious education for the bazaars, in turn, used the religious taxes received from well-to-do bazaaris to provide personalized welfare services for the devout urban poor.

The secular National Front also made attempts to help the poor mobilize against the shah. The task was made easier after it made an explicit tactical alliance with the religious groups to topple the regime. In fact, after calling the monarchy illegal, many of the National Front leaders held meetings and rallies in the migrant poor areas of South Tehran. There is, however, no doubt that the religious hierarchy was logistically in a much better position to reach the poor and address their grievances. In their attempt to entice the urban poor to join peaceful demonstrations, the mosques and the bazaars were particularly effective in using elaborate rituals of the Shi'ite religious processions, with all their emotional trappings.[22] The result, as Kazemi reports, was that the mobilized response of the migrant poor was overwhelmingly in religious terms: "Whether in the form of shouting *Allahu Akbar* (God Almighty) from rooftops at night or facing the Shah's military forces head-on in the streets of Tehran, the religious dimension remained the dominant mode of expression for the migrant poor."[23]

Yet it is also important to note that, during normal periods, the organizational and cultural links developed by the religious hierarchy were limited to nonpolitical activities. Governmental control of these communities was simply too overwhelming to allow for political activities. However, as the state became engulfed in a confrontation with the more economically prominent classes and hence was forced to loosen its grip over civil society, these links were used to mobilize the urban poor, especially in the nonsquatting communities. The mobilization of the squatters was more difficult since their concerns over day-to-day survival prevented them from sustained antiregime activities.[24]

The relationship between the state and the workers in large industries was much more controlled. Of course, in some cases, like the oil company, the state was the employer. The approach to these workers was Janus-faced. On the one hand, the state dealt severely with any kind of independent collective activity (economic or political) on the part of the workers. The unions were sanctioned by the government, the structures were run directly by SAVAK, and attempted strikes were dealt with severely.[25] On the other hand, the regime was careful to entice the workers by providing a number of welfare schemes related to insurance, housing, and pensions as well as such symbolic benefits as profit-sharing industry and, later, share participation. In addition, the government itself continued to adjust the minimum wage (without any threat of strikes) and supervised large industries in carrying out these wage increases. In short, as one observer has pointed out, the regime attempted to structure relationships with the working class "from above without politically activating them."[26]

The relationship between the state and workers had important consequences. Clearly, an independent working-class movement was severely inhibited. The feared SAVAK was never able totally to prevent industrial strikes, but it did a pretty good job. More important, by directly inserting itself into the employer-employee relationship, the state made itself indispensable to the smooth functioning of that relationship. At the same time, the state became the sole object of grievances, which increased as the oil boom turned into a bust when the government was forced to pursue recessionary policies to cool down an overheated economy.

It is important to reiterate that the brief analysis of the subordinate classes points to certain significant factors inhibiting autonomous and collective action, despite the increase in grievances. First, during the period after the land reform, these communities were being polarized from within by, on the one hand, the rise of the relatively well-off industrial working class and, on the other hand, many migrants' decline into poverty or insecurity. Second, as if such socioeconomic impediments were not enough, the ruthless and cooptative manner (depending on the situation) in which the regime dealt with political activities severely inhibited independent movements.

This is why it was only after June 1978 that the urban wage earners, especially construction laborers and factory workers, started to join the revolutionary forces in massive numbers. Before June, as Ervand Abrahamian reports, the urban wage earners, with the exception of the ones in Tabriz, had been conspicuous by their absence.[27] Most demonstrators had been drawn from the ranks of the intermediate classes. The revolutionary political crisis of the state—itself occasioned by developments independent of urban wage earners—was the factor that created conditions favorable to their massive entry into the revolutionary scene.

In the case of workers in large industrial factories, the crisis of the state brought about a weakening of state-controlled unions and opened the way for a multitude of industrial strikes, culminating in a strike by oil workers in September of 1978 that paralyzed the economy.[28] At this time, factory workers also became actively involved in street demonstrations. In general, according to Assef Bayat, the activities of workers, especially in the strike movement, were coordinated by grass-roots leadership within the workplace. Outside influences from left-wing, urban guerrilla groups (like the Marxist-oriented Fedayin-e Khalq and the Islamic-oriented Mojahedin-e Khalq) and the Tudeh party became widespread only during the Bakhtiar government, when the conditions for open political agitation were realized. Even then, despite gaining control over a large amount of armament, the leftist groups and parties were unable to make lasting inroads. The organizational linkages created were simply too recent to allow radical groups to orchestrate and sustain significant mobilization of the workers. The result was important autonomy for the workers but also a noticeable weakness since "no effective initiatives were taken by the workers to unify and coordinate the [de facto strike] committees; no central strike fund was established."[29]

In the case of the rest of urban wage earners, their lack of internal organization was rapidly replaced by traditional channels of communication as the bazaar guilds, religious sessions, mosques, and coffee houses provided the necessary linkages between the traditional intermediate class and the urban poor. It was precisely these cultural and organizational channels that made the political ascent of the clergy possible in the postrevolutionary period.

Urban Life and Revolution in Nicaragua

As in Iran, the Nicaraguan urban landscape was influenced by drastic changes in the countryside. The changes in Nicaragua, however, were not directly introduced by state policy. Rather, it was the increased penetration of agroexports that brought the proletarianization of some of the peasants in the countryside and the artisans in the cities, as well as the displacement of others, all of whom were incorporated into the large surplus labor force crowding the central cities in each region (Managua, Masaya, León, and Estelí).[30]

In the countryside, although a relatively large number of peasants (about 30 percent of the economically active population—EAP—in agriculture) continued to be producers, the extent of proletarianization was actually more advanced than in the cities. The economy's dependence on a few export crops clearly contributed to an increasingly salaried work force in the rural areas. Given the harvest calendar and the cyclical demand for labor power, however, many workers were forced to seek other occupations or to endure periods of unemployment. Carlos Vilas estimates that toward the end of the 1970s the agricultural proletariat constituted about one-third of the agricultural EAP, with more than 60 percent of them having fixed employment for only two or three months a year. For "the rest of the year they functioned as an *itinerant proletariat* that once the cotton and coffee harvest season had passed, moved to urban services, construction or whatever, generally maintaining their salaried conditions."[31] Another one-third of the agricultural EAP, while not fully in the salaried category, were nevertheless unable to live from the products of their farm (owned or rented) and hence were obliged to sell their labor power to other producers. Proletarianization and the need to go to the cities for at least part of the year meant that the clear line between the city and countryside, based on the difference in the relationship to the means of production and geographical separation, had begun to blur.[32]

In the cities themselves, the process of proletarianization was less advanced, but it nevertheless added to the complexity of the urban landscape. According to Vilas, who has provided the most extensive analysis of the Nicaraguan class structure to date, by the end of 1970s "the urban working class was about 113,000 workers (in industry, construction, transport, energy production, and assimilated industries), or 20 percent of the nonagricultural EAP."[33] Vilas goes on to say:

This small industrial working class was highly dispersed in the urban socio-economic landscape, living together with a mass of nonsalaried, or salaried but nonproductive workers, which easily surpassed them in both relative and absolute terms. Approximately one-third of the nonagricultural EAP (some 150,000 people) consisted of nonproductive workers— administrative employees in the private and public sectors, salaried informal sector workers, and so on—and almost 40 percent consisted of artisans, petty merchants, tradespeople, and in general self-employed or non-remunerated family workers in the petty production and petty property sector.[34]

Following this logic, Vilas can say that the urban experience had a tendency to obscure the separation between the laboring class and the nonproletarianized workers. This is true especially since, given the low wages, many of the minor or female members of the proletarian families were forced to contribute to family income by engaging in unsalaried activities (e.g., shoe-shining, watching cars, and selling food). In general, the urban experience was a difficult one for everybody. The difficulty became even more pronounced after the 1972 earthquake in Managua. In addition to the thousands of dead and injured, the catastrophe left more than 50,000 people without work and displaced some 250,000 people— 60 percent of the total population of Managua.[35] With 75 percent of family housing units destroyed, many middle- and low-income families were left in the street without housing, work, and personal belongings.

This desolate socioeconomic condition, however, did not fully disrupt the process of community-building within many of the urban slums. Although information is not available for all the poor settlements, it is clear a strong sense of community existed among at least some of them. George Black's description of the Indian barrio of Monimbo is a good example:

> The Indians of Monimbo have . . . made the city the craft center of Nicaragua. The livelihood of the barrio rests on the production of embroidered clothes, *marimbas* and other musical instruments, wooden toys and carved hand-painted gourds. The barrio also had a highly developed sense of community and a unique geography. Between fifteen and twenty thousand people live in an area which contains a number of smaller sectors. . . . Earth yards are a common feature of poor houses throughout Nicaragua, but nowhere else do they all interconnect as they do in Monimbo. To the stranger—as it was to the National Guard—Monimbo is a confusing warren of narrow earth streets and wooden or adobe houses. But to the *monimbosenos*, every inch is familiar territory which, when the insurrection came, allowed easy communication as well as easy escape for the combatants.[36]

These local conditions were instrumental in bringing about the insurrection that, after Chamorro's assassination, began "spontaneously with barricades, but was quickly taken over with more systematic organization by the people themselves, block by block and house by house throughout the barrio."[37] The ethnic and economic cohesiveness existing in Monimbo was not present in many other poor settlements, but there were other sources of cohesion. For instance, although, unlike the Iranian case, the church hierarchy had not been involved in organizing urban communities, after the 1968 Latin American Bishops' Conference in Medellín, Colombia, and especially after the Managua earthquake, many of the lower clerics and lay Catholics began helping the poor combat adverse conditions. Rather than operating within the hierarchical framework of the church, Catholic religious orders organized hundreds of study groups, youth clubs, and "Christian base communities," in the cities as well as the countryside, to promote spiritual growth through social action and community improvement and to put pressure on the government for better social services.[38]

The Nicaraguan religious organizations differed from their Iranian counterparts in at least two ways. First, their task of social improvement put them directly at odds with the Somoza regime since it was undertaken precisely in the arena the state had failed so miserably. Yet, and this is the second reason, they never developed a project to vie for state power, as will be shown more fully in the next chapter. In other words, the radicalism of the grass-roots church was mostly related to the impoverished condition of the poor. The religious activists saw their task as one of improving social conditions through community work, not organizing to overthrow the regime.

These two differences created conditions in which religious organizations could easily cooperate with another organization also interested in mobilizing the poor—the FSLN.[39] In fact, according to John A. Booth, the "clerics working in poor barrios, in the countryside, or with university and high school students became contact points between the FSLN and the Christian neighborhood organizations throughout Nicaragua."[40] Having community bases, these Christian groups provided key organizational resources for the guerrillas, performing tasks ranging from raising money to stockpiling food and medical supplies. These resources were put to the service of the FSLN partly because, as mentioned, the Christian clerics were not competitors for state power. More important, these resources were given to the Sandinistas because in the 1970s they were the only organized political group with roots in the urban barrios.

The FSLN had originated as an isolated organization committed to a Cuban-type, rural-guerrilla strategy.[41] Its membership was mostly drawn from students with middle-class backgrounds. In 1967, they even engaged in a series of armed raids in the countryside, using both peasant and urban cadres, which brought the name of the FSLN into the Nicaraguan political consciousness. Severe military defeats by the National Guard and increasing popular discontent in the cities, however, prompted the organization to reorient. Instead of taking direct military action, the FSLN set about strengthening its links with the people. Because it was forced to operate underground, it created "intermediate organizations," connected to the FSLN but not bearing its name. The Sandinistas carried out intense organizing efforts in the factories and poor barrios, winning over many members of the Nicaraguan Socialist party. In the universities, the Student Revolutionary Front (FER) became a major force. According to Gary Ruchwarger, "The FER and other intermediate organizations put forth FSLN demands in communities and work sites, presenting—to the extent conditions permitted—the political line of the underground leadership. Furthermore, each time the National Guard lashed out at the FSLN these organizations led demonstrations to protest the Guard's repression."[42]

It is important to note that the FSLN never gave up its rural strategy, but political and military circumstances made such a strategy difficult if not impossible until later.[43] In 1974, after an audacious and successful FSLN military raid, Somoza unleashed a state of siege that effectively controlled the activities of the FSLN combatants and militants. More important, as Black reports, Somoza's reign of terror prevented sectors of the FSLN operating in different locations from making contact with each other, and rational, unified discussions on future strategy became impossible.[44] The result was an open rift among three separate tendencies, variously favoring emphasis on the creation of a vanguard urban proletarian party, a guerrilla strategy centered on the rural proletariat, or a mass insurrection strategy made possible by the development of a coalition against Somoza that included the opposition bourgeoisie.[45]

All this meant that, during the critical period of the state of siege, the bourgeois opposition had far more room to maneuver than the Sandinistas did. The FSLN, plagued with dissension and suffering from leadership depletion caused by imprisonment and combat deaths, was constantly forced to restructure. The bourgeois opposition's major move to oppose the regime was the creation of the Democratic Union for Liberation (UDEL), which was a coalition of reformist political and trade union groups with no clear political program. Headed by the charismatic Pedro Joaquín Chamorro, the coalition did have a leadership with genuine popular appeal in the country. However, UDEL's lack of political clarity prevented it from becoming the leader of all oppositional forces. This lack of clarity was essentially caused by disagreements over the future of Nicaragua once Somoza was gone.[46] As a result, UDEL limited itself to an electoral strategy and hoped for negotiation with Somoza. In many ways the bourgeois opposition had no other choice. Its own complicity with the Somoza regime for so many years, and Somoza's ruthless crushing of all significant political activities, prevented the formation of the organizational links necessary to tap Chamorro's popularity and to make UDEL a "true" alternative to Somoza.

This is why Chamorro's assassination, rather than creating sympathy support for UDEL, opened the way for large numbers of Nicaraguans to join the insurrectional process. To be sure, in an attempt to maintain the leadership of the struggle, the church hierarchy, traditional opposition parties, and the business community called for massive nationwide demonstrations and a general strike. But in less than a month isolated protests and revolts began to merge and identify themselves as Sandinista. The FSLN then had to unite the opposition and develop a strong national organization to conduct a coherent military and political war against a regime that was politically isolated but still had enough military firepower to cause serious damage.

In many ways, this was a task for which the FSLN leadership was not fully prepared. Many of the leaders within the FSLN had thus far insisted that an insurrection, without the presence of strong mass organization led by the FSLN, would only benefit Somoza's conservative opponents and the United States, by then eager to replace Somoza. But the divisions within the bourgeois opposition allowed the ascent of a political position advocated by some FSLN leaders, who argued that revolutionary forces could gain hegemony within a broad, anti-Somoza coalition. A national political organization, called the United People's Movement (MPU) was thus created in August 1978, *after* the January and February riots in various urban barrios. This organization brought all opposition forces together and projected a national alternative to Somoza. In addition, a network of underground local cells paralleling local power structures was created by using the already existing linkages developed through intermediate organizations and religious connections. These barrio-based organizations fused political work and military preparation and began to prepare for the final encounter with Somoza's forces. Given Somoza's intransigence and the National Guard's isolation, the encounter was much more violent than its Iranian counterpart, but it also ended with the downfall of a dictator.

Summing Up

The examination of the urban landscape and revolutionary uprisings in Iran and Nicaragua tends to reinforce the theoretical propositions presented in chapter 1. It has shown that urbanization in Iran and Nicaragua led to the increasing intervention of the state in the urban process. As the "manager of the means of daily life," the Iranian and Nicaraguan states became the guardians as well as the nemeses of the urban poor. On the one hand, the urban poor became highly dependent on their generosity; on the other hand, they feared them and found them responsible for their grievances. With the weakening of these states, the clientelist relationships and the laboriously developed networks of repression began to disintegrate. This allowed for the revolutionary mobilization of the urban poor by organizations linked to other social groupings.

Two points need to be mentioned about this type of mobilization. First, it is important to stress that this type of mobilization was not an automatic reflection of state disintegration. Several elements intervened to forge revolutionary links between subordinate classes and external organizations. In Iran, the most important was that these organizations already had nonpolitical networks operating within poor urban communities, and these in time were transformed into political ones. In Nicaragua, the ability of the FSLN to develop strategic alliances was aided by the work of Christian base communities and other intermediate organizations. In any case, what all this means is that, like the peasants' involvement in China, the urban poor's contribution to the Iranian and Nicaraguan revolutions resembled much more of a mobilized response to a revolutionary elite's initiatives than did the peasant contributions in France and Russia. Even in Nicaragua, where spontaneous riots did occur and in fact were instrumental in pushing the revolutionary leadership toward insurrection, the ability of the FSLN to capitalize on these riots and to direct a national strategy against Somoza was made possible by the work it had already done within urban barrios. However, and this is the second point that needs to be made, the linkages created between the external organizations and mobilized forces, unlike those in China, were not based on bonds between an organized revolutionary party and the subordinate classes. In fact, the revolutionary party that came to dominate the postrevolutionary scene was not fully developed until the last stages of the struggle in Iran and Nicaragua. Linkages were made possible by organizational and cultural forms of social communication already existing in urban communities. Even in Nicaragua, where bonds had been more recently created, the FSLN did not enter urban communities as a political party and attract support on that basis. Instead, it operated through local or intermediate organizations embedded in, and respectful of, everyday practices and beliefs of the people. This is why attention is now turned to the manner in which these practices and beliefs were reproduced and transformed to understand their contribution to revolutionary processes in Iran and Nicaragua.

NOTES

1. A. Portes, "Rationality in the Slum: An Essay on Interpretive Sociology," *Comparative Studies in Society and History* 14 (June 1972), pp. 268–86; W. Cornelius, Jr., *Politics and the Migrant Poor in Mexico City* (Palo Alto, Calif.: Stanford University Press, 1975); J. Perlman, *The Myth of Marginality: Urban Poverty and Politics in Rio de Janeiro* (Berkeley: University of California Press, 1976); F. Kazemi, *Poverty and Revolution in Iran: The Migrant Poor, Urban Marginality and Politics* (New York: New York University Press, 1980).

2. C. Tilly, *From Mobilization to Revolution* (Reading, Mass.: Addison-Wesley, 1978).

3. J. Gugler, "The Urban Character of Contemporary Revolutions," *Studies in Comparative and International Development* 17 (Summer 1982), p. 67.

4. The emphasis on autonomy and shared understanding here is similar to Skocpol's focus on autonomy and solidarity in peasant communities; however, there is an important difference. For Skocpol, peasant autonomy is explained in terms of independence from owners/controllers of the means of production. Within the urban setting, autonomy is expressed in relation to the center of state power. For a detailed analysis of the uses, as well as limitations, of Skocpol's analysis in relation to the urban context, see F. Farhi, "State-Disintegration and Urban-Based Revolutionary Crisis: The Iranian Case" (Ph.D. dissertation, University of Colorado, 1986), pp. 77–82.

5. See especially C. J. Calhoun, "Radicalism of Tradition and the Question of Class Struggle," in *Rationality and Revolution*, ed. M. Taylor (Cambridge: Cambridge University Press, 1988), pp. 129–75. By traditional, Calhoun does not mean a way of life generated in antiquity and communicated across generations. Rather, a traditional community sustains itself as members "in manifold interactions produce and reproduce shared understandings of their behavior." Ibid., p. 146.

6. Ibid., pp. 153–54.

7. The urban nature of the protest movements has generally been traced to the existence of independent social groupings—the bazaar classes, the ulama, and the intellectuals—vis-à-vis the state in the cities as well as to the nonrevolutionary character of the peasantry. On the former, see N. Keddie, "Class Structure and Political Power in Iran since 1796," *Iranian Studies* 11, 4 (1978), pp. 305–30, and H. Katouzian, "The Aridisolatic Society: A Model of Long-Term Social and Economic Development in Iran," *International Journal of Middle East Studies* 15, 2 (1983), pp. 259–81. On the latter, see N. Keddie, "Stratification, Social Control, and Capitalism in Iranian Villages: Before and after Land Reform," in *Rural Politics and Social Change in the Middle East*, ed. I. Harik and R. Antoun (Bloomington: Indiana University Press, 1972), and F. Kazemi and E. Abrahamian, "The Non-Revolutionary Peasantry of Modern Iran," *Iranian Studies* 11, 4 (1978), pp. 259–303.

8. Hooglund also reports that the preponderant majority of rural migrants were young men. He estimates that the number of migrants to the cities between 1966 and 1976 hovered close to three million people. The greatest impact was on the largest cities, especially Tehran, Isfahan, and Mashhad. E. J. Hooglund, *Land and Revolution in Iran, 1960–1980* (Austin: University of Texas Press, 1982), pp. 115–21.

9. See ibid.; H. Katouzian, "Land Reform in Iran: A Case Study in the Political Economy of Social Engineering," *Journal of Peasant Studies* 1 (January 1974), pp. 220–39; and Kazemi, *Poverty and Revolution in Iran*, pp. 32–42.

10. Hooglund, *Land and Revolution in Iran*, p. 115.

11. On this, see E. Hooglund, "The Khwushnishin Population of Iran," *Iranian Studies* 6 (August 1973), pp. 229–45.

12. Close to one million people were employed by the construction industry by 1977. This constituted approximately 15 percent of the urban labor force. See F. Halliday, *Iran: Dictatorship and Development* (New York: Penguin, 1979), p. 176.

13. Hooglund, *Land and Revolution in Iran*, p. 118.

14. Halliday, *Iran*, pp. 181–83.

15. Kazemi, *Poverty and Revolution in Iran*, pp. 55–59.

16. Ibid.

17. E. Abrahamian, *Iran: Between Two Revolutions* (Princeton, N.J.: Princeton University Press, 1982), p. 484.

18. This section on the urban poor is based on Kazemi's empirical work on such communities. See Kazemi, *Poverty and Revolution in Iran*.

19. Ibid., p. 62.

20. Ibid., p. 63.

21. Ibid.

22. For a revealing study of how this was done, see M. J. Fischer, *Iran: From Religious Dispute to Revolution* (Cambridge, Mass.: Harvard University Press, 1980).

23. Kazemi, *Poverty and Revolution in Iran*, p. 95.

24. It is worth mentioning that one of the first expressions of grievances occurred when a crowd of squatters, whose quarters had been demolished by the police, set out from south of Tehran to the shah's palace in the northern part of the city. These efforts, however, were directly related to their basic needs and survival. The nonsquatting settlers were much more politically motivated. Ibid., pp. 95–96.

25. Halliday, *Iran*, pp. 202–5.

26. H. Bashiriyeh, *State and Revolution in Iran, 1962–1982* (New York: St. Martin's Press, 1984), p. 43.

27. Abrahamian, *Iran*, pp. 510–24. For a more detailed discussion of the activities of the industrial working class, see A. Bayat, *Workers and Revolution in Iran* (London: Zed Press, 1987), chapter 6.

28. The wave of strikes closed down not only many of the oil refineries but also most of the oil fields.

29. Bayat, *Workers and Revolution in Iran*, p. 94.

30. By the time of the revolution, close to 54 percent of the population lived in the urban areas. This was the highest in Central America. See J. Weeks, *The Economies of Central America* (New York: Holmes and Meier, 1985), p. 42, table 3. Between 1950 and 1971, the city of Managua alone quadrupled its population, going from less than 110,000 inhabitants to almost 400,000. See C. M. Vilas, *The Sandinista Revolution* (New York: Monthly Review Press, 1986), p. 101.

31. Vilas, *The Sandinista Revolution*, p. 63.

32. The high proportion of seasonally unemployed agricultural workers in the cities casts some doubt on the centrality and meaning of *urban* in Nicaragua as compared to Iran. In this study, however, I am not denying the importance of the rural connection, which, in the case of Nicaragua, was fully maintained because of seasonal work. I am simply suggesting that the confrontation with the regime was being carried out mostly in the urban areas and thus the urban landscape made an important difference. In other words, in this chapter, the communities created to sustain rural migrants are given more weight than class origins.

33. Vilas, *The Sandinista Revolution*, p. 66.

34. Ibid., p. 68.

35. Ibid., pp. 102–3.

36. G. Black, *Triumph of the People: The Sandinista Revolution in Nicaragua* (London: Zed Press, 1981), p. 113.

37. Ibid., p. 114.

38. The context within which the ideological shift that made this change of approach within the religious community possible will be discussed in the next chapter.

39. For a succinct and informative history of the FSLN, see Black, *Triumph of the People*, chapter 6.

40. J. A. Booth, *The End and the Beginning: The Nicaraguan Revolution* (Boulder, Colo.: Westview Press, 1982), p. 136.

41. More on the ideological formation of the FSLN in the next chapter.

42. G. Ruchwarger, *People in Power* (South Hadley, Mass.: Bergin & Garvey, 1987), p. 16.

43. Of course, the FSLN later scored major successes in the countryside. The Rural Workers Association (ATC), promoted by the FSLN and staffed by the members of a rural pastoral program, was involved in extensive and effective organization of the peasantry and agricultural workers by early 1978.

44. Black, *Triumph of the People*, p. 91.

45. Originally, there was a two-way split between those favoring emphasis on political, educational, and agitational work with urban working-class cadres and marginal barrio-dwellers and those favoring a prolonged rural offensive. The third force emerged when members of the FSLN leadership in exile attempted to reconcile the two positions and soon came up with their own "insurrectionist" strategy, favoring cooperation with all sectors of the society to overthrow Somoza.

46. Disagreements were only natural within a coalition that included Conservative and Liberal party dissidents as well as the Moscow-line Nicaraguan Socialist Party (PSN). Not surprisingly, Conservative members wanted little more than cosmetic reforms, while the PSN called for the nationalization of all Somoza's property.

4

The Role of Ideology

We have to get rid of selfishness and do what Christ said, and
go on with the Revolution, as you socialists say. I'm not a
socialist, I'm not a revolutionary. I like to hear the talk and
grasp what I can but really I'm nothing. Although I would like
to see a change in Nicaragua.

—Pancho, as recorded in gospel
discussions at Solentiname

As I suggested in chapter 1, the question the role ideology plays in
mass mobilization for sociopolitical change is an important one, requiring theoretical rethinking as well as an understanding of how particular
ideologies are created and transformed historically.[1] I deal with the latter
in separate sections on the histories of Islamic activism in its Iranian
version and Sandinista socialism. At this point, however, it is important
to elaborate on some of the theoretical presuppositions that underlie the
writing of this chapter.

The most important presupposition is the rejection of ideology as a
system of ideas. Instead, ideology is conceived as a dynamic, ongoing
social process through which subjects are created and yet, at the same
time, is subject to transformation by the willful actions of more or less
knowledgeable actors. Following Göran Therborn, ideology is "that aspect
of the human condition under which human beings live their lives as
conscious actors in a world that makes sense to them to varying degrees."[2]
Hence, ideology must be understood by aligning it not with consciously
held political beliefs but with the large cultural systems that preceded it
and out of which, as well as against which, it came into being.

This does not mean that there are no distinctions between culture
and ideology. Real cultures entail diverse, often conflicting symbols,
stories, rituals, and world views from which actors select different strategies for action.[3] Ideologies, on the other hand, are highly articulated

cultural models aspiring to offer one unified answer to the question of how human beings should live and act. As such, they are produced to alter the existing world views and assumptions. Yet even during ideologically charged periods, as Ann Swidler points out, they are deeply connected to the cultures in which they are embedded. This is because "rather than providing the underlying assumptions of an entire way of life, they make explicit demands in a contested cultural arena. Their independent cultural influence is limited . . . because, at least at their origins, such ideological movements are not complete cultures, in the sense that much of their taken-for-granted understanding of the world and many of their daily practices still depend on traditional patterns."[4]

Of course, over time, ideology may deepen its critique of the existing order and begin to unsettle even the taken-for-granted areas of everyday life. But important linkages to the old cultural order remain that need to be investigated to shed light on the available strategies of action. After all, if we accept that the notion of culture is a "tool-kit" of diverse strategies for action, then we must accept that the existing cultural order also qualifies people to "take up and perform the repertoire of roles given in the society into which they are born, including the role of possible agents of social change."[5]

During periods of rapid social change, cultural meanings wear the mask of ideology as they become highly articulated and explicit to promote patterns of action that are easily perceived. This process, which Therborn calls ideological mobilization, involves:

> setting a common agenda for a mass of people—that is to say, summing up the dominant aspect or aspects of the crisis, identifying the crucial target, the essence of evil, and defining what is possible and how it should be achieved. Such mobilization develops through a breach in the regime's matrix of affirmations and sanctions, which in normal times ensures compromise or acquiescence and the successful sanctioning of oppositional forces. This breach grows to the extent that it is itself successfully affirmed in the practice of demonstrations, acts of insubordination and revolt, and so on. A successful ideological mobilization is always translated or manifested in practices of political mobilization.[6]

This does not mean that the process of ideological mobilization is self-consistent. Rather, it is generally imbued with contradictory and antagonistic actions by a large number of actors or groups of actors. But successful ideological mobilization always manages to fuse and condense several ideological discourses into a single major theme, usually expressed in a single slogan. For our purposes, the interesting question relates to the process through which certain groups become the "real" articulators of this major theme. We thus need to understand how, given the existing cultural models, a particular highly organized meaning system (let us say, secular as opposed to religious) gains currency and why one ideology, as well as the particular social groupings associated with it, triumphs rather than another. This is a task that can be accomplished only through the historical analysis of particular cases.

Concrete historical forms of ideological mobilization have given us clues about several sources the revolutionaries can draw on to mobilize. The most important source seems to be the "dangerous" memory of conflict and exclusion.[7] This memory has two dimensions: suffering as well as resistance and hope. The former draws from concrete memories of specific histories of oppression and suffering. "It declares that such suffering matters; the oppression of the people is of ultimate concern."[8] Past suffering hence becomes an indictment of existing economic and political systems. Memory of resistance and hope, on the other hand, chronicles actual or imagined instances of resistance and liberation. These accounts are a declaration of the possibility of change, and they are examined continuously in an attempt to understand what enables resistance in specific, historical situations. They are also generally reenacted in symbolic fashion through plays, sermons, religious ceremonies, and the like to sustain the revolutionary fervor. The ultimate result is the creation and sustenance of "the memory of a community in which people were freed to claim an identity from that imposed on them. It is both a memory of past liberation and a motivation for further liberation. It is a memory of resistance and of hope for further resistance."[9]

It is important to point out that the "true" retrieval and propagation of an actual event is not at issue here. Rather, it is the process of *imagining* and *creating* the memory of the struggles that matters. To be sure, the particular memory of suffering and resistance may be connected to an actual event, but it is the manner in which that event is constructed that ultimately becomes a source for mobilization. This is why the historical context of the event itself (at least in terms of time and geography) is not relevant in the creation of the memory. The memory of resistance, as in the case of Iran, may draw from a timeless past, a past that reportedly witnessed the martyrdom of a religious leader in his attempt to institute the true, just Islamic society. Or, as in the case of Nicaragua, the memory may go beyond the geographical and national boundaries and draw from the experiences of other people perceived to be in similar situation (i.e., Cuba). In all cases, the memory itself is dynamic insofar as it changes with the deepening of the revolutionary crisis.

Why do certain memories of exclusion and conflict begin to attract a large audience during the revolutionary process? After all, there are Christian-based liberation movements in most of Latin America and more or less radical Islam in countries from Nigeria to the Philippines. What explains the success of Islamic activism in Iran and the Christian-Marxist dialogue in Nicaragua? The central premise of this chapter is that the answer to this question is twofold. On the one hand, I argue that the imagination and creation of "dangerous" memory as well as the particular vision of the future must be understood as they emerge from the ruins of the prerevolutionary ideological structures. This is because ideological mobilization always entails two processes: the decomposition of the old and the recomposition of the new one.[10] These are interrelated processes because the old ideological structures define certain possibilities and impossibilities. A close look at the ideological glue that held the old regime together is thus important not only to understand the contradictions that unraveled the ideological hold of the old regime but also to lay out the recomposition of the new ideological system.

On the other hand, emerging ideologies cannot be seen merely as reactions. Important independent organizational and ideational mutations occurred within the oppositional movements of both Iran and Nicaragua that must be examined. These mutations were historically specific, but their interaction with the old ideological structure created an explosive chemistry not present in other places. As will be shown in the following sections, the old ideological structures prevented the success of secular ideologies in Iran and the liberal solution in Nicaragua, while the particular histories of the oppositional movements helped to bring forth increasing radicalism in both countries.

The Ideologies of Prerevolutionary Regimes

The ideological foundations of the Iranian and Nicaraguan prerevolutionary regimes were complex and contradictory. As in most peripheral formations, the complexities and contradictions were related to the disjunctions between the structure and behavior of the prerevolutionary states and the two important ideological discourses that accompanied their respective modern state formation: modernization (economic as well as political) and nationalism. The undemocratic (and in many ways archaic) structure of these states and their emergence through the defeat of nationalist forces clearly contrasted with the image they felt obligated to portray. Accordingly, both regimes developed fairly complex sets of arguments and symbols to account for and camouflage this disparity. Ultimately, however, like the other social structures, these ideological webs failed, allowing other ideological forces to mobilize. The particular contexts leading to the failures were different and are important for understanding the process of ideological struggle.

The ideological foundation of the Iranian regime had two components: official nationalism[11] and the defense of the monarchy as the true representative of progressive/modernizing/democratizing forces. The official nationalism of Mohammad Reza Pahlavi developed after the defeat of the oil nationalization movement in the 1950s. To gain legitimacy, the shah's regime coopted much of the language and issues used by the nationalist movements. Control over oil production and profits thus became an ideological cornerstone of the new regime. Not only did the shah not denationalize the oil industry but he portrayed himself as the champion of the Iranian cause. This was despite the fact that Iranian oil production and exports effectively remained in the hands of foreigners until the 1970s.[12] Once fundamental changes did occur in the patterns of control through the coordinated pressure of the Organization of Petroleum Exporting Countries (OPEC), much was made of the shah's leadership role in bringing about that change.

Much was also made of Iran's embarking on the path of industrialization. In fact, the language of progress slowly began to replace the nationalist discourse. If Iran were going to "catch up with the West soon," then there was no contradiction between Iranian national aspirations and the close relationship developed with the West in general and the United States in particular. It was not foreign control that held Iran back, official rhetoric implied, but the lack of proper technology, skills, attitudes, and ideas—all of which could be bought or copied from the West. Iran, unlike many other peripheral formations, could overcome the hurdle of backwardness because of oil revenues and its long and distinguished past. I have already mentioned how oil had become connected to nationalism. The reference to Iranian history, however, requires more elaboration since it relates to the anti-Islamic bent of the regime.

Modern Iranian political thought had been preoccupied with the issue of nationalism since the end of nineteenth century.[13] Any summary does injustice to the complexity of debates within modern Iranian political theory, but it is fair to say that the relationship of Iranian nationalism to Islam was the most contentious part of the debate. Some theorists called for unity around Islam to fend off the West. Others rejected Islam by interpreting Iranian history as one of defeat, passivity, and corruption after Islam and the "inferior" Arabs "conquered" Iran. These writers looked to the great pre-Islamic Persian empires for nationalist inspiration. As Nikki Keddie points out, both Islamic and anti-Islamic nationalisms were multiclass phenomena, but it was the latter that was picked up by the Pahlavi dynasty.[14] Keddie also gives the best explanation for why this interpretation of the Iranian past, at least for a while, was not contested:

The Pahlavi Shahs picked-up pre-Islamic Iranian nationalism, cut-off the radical elements that were central to its chief intellectual advocates (especially the communist religion and revolt of the fifth-century A.D. heretic Mazdak), and made it a foundation of anticlerical monarchism. This use of it was probably no more forced than the other, as the two great pre-Islamic empires were strong monarchies; on the other hand popular elements could be found in pre-Islamic religions like Mazdakism, Manichaeism, and Zoroastrianism, as could evidence that women and agriculturalists enjoyed higher respect in some pre-Islamic periods than in the nineteenth century. The main appeal of an idealized distant past, however, whether Islamic or pre-Islamic, was and is that a great variety of values may be read into it, while the evils of the present can be ascribed to deviation from the true Iranian and true Islamic essence. In a period when all society was at least formally Islamic, it was natural for many thinkers to blame Iran's problems on Islam and the Arabs, and to see in a nationalist interpretation of the distant Iranian past virtues that were often modern or Western ones.[15]

This use of pre-Islamic Iranian history also lent itself to the defense of monarchy as a proper method of rule. The Pahlavi dynasty, since it had usurped power relatively recently, did not benefit from the blood lineage that usually gives legitimacy to hereditary rule. Instead, it tried to represent itself as the "true" heir of the "glorious" Persian tradition; hence, the task of the monarchy was portrayed as one of reestablishing Iranian greatness in the international arena. No longer was the monarchy to be perceived as an archaic institution. Rather, its mission was to modernize Iran. If its monarchical form did not seem particularly modern, it had less to do with the desires and actions of the monarch—who was presumably a democrat at heart—and more to do with the exigencies of backwardness in Iran. After all, what would be more progressive and democratic than redistributing land to peasants, extending suffrage to women, and creating a national literacy corps, all instituted by royal decree during the White Revolution (later renamed the Shah-People Revolution) in the 1960s. These policies were complemented with the almost daily repetition and celebration of the monarch's role in "civilizing" Iran. The attempt was to create an almost god-like image for him.[16] God-like because it represented the monarch as the creator of modern Iran as well as a body to be feared. Ironically, the success of this ideological construction ultimately proved problematic. The shah was accepted as the creator, but he was also seen as responsible for the results. He was feared, but he was also loathed. In other words, it was the thinness of the lines separating creation from responsibility and fear from hatred that opened the way for the possibility of ideological opposition in Iran.

In Nicaragua, the Somoza family was less successful in maintaining a sophisticated justification for family rule. This is why it ultimately had to rely on overt repression to survive. The family's, and especially Anastasio Somoza Debayle's, systematic pillage of the nation's wealth was simply too difficult to hide or justify through ideological pronouncements. Nevertheless, the family did try. For instance, as Henri Weber aptly points out, "under certain obligations as a member of 'the free world', the dynastic regime did not bedeck itself in the forms of monarchy or hereditary dictatorship, but paraded all the trappings of 'democracy'."[17] Elections, although fully rigged, were regularly held. Various Somozas also diligently worked around, instead of completely ignoring, the constitutional ban on indefinite reappointment to presidential office. Weber best explains how this was done: "For half a century, the Somozas circumvented this provision either by means of constitutional changes or by the classical Latin American technique of *continuismo:* they organized the election of a puppet who would hand back the presidency after a brief lap of honour. During the 42-year reign of the Somozas, five such marionettes would assume the land's highest office for a total of just over three and a half years."[18]

Another component of the discourse of democracy was the maintenance of the party system. To be sure, popular parties were prohibited for espousing unacceptable ideologies, but the Conservative party and two smaller parties with similar disposition were tolerated insofar as they did not pose a threat to the family. In 1972, Anastasio Somoza Debayle even allowed the Conservative party to share power in almost every branch of the government as a reward for its complicity in the practice of continuismo. Real power sharing was the farthest thing from Somoza's mind, and this arrangement predictably did not increase the effective power of the Conservative party as an oppositional force. In fact, the results were the opposite. Collaboration with the regime alienated many members and splintered the party. The effect was even more dramatic among the younger Conservatives. Many renounced conservatism entirely for much more radical alternatives. By continuing to flirt with the language of democracy, Somoza had in fact discredited attempts to bring about democratic practices through reformist politics.

The Somoza family's usage of anticommunism as a justification for its control also had ironic results. The family's denotation of any real opposition as communist clearly had two audiences. On the one hand, it was an important tool in maintaining U.S. support at any cost. On the other hand, it was a useful reminder to the emerging intermediate classes and the bourgeoisie that, despite excesses, the family did maintain a good business climate. The indiscriminate use of the term, however, simply went too far. After a while, the term did not refer to an opponent of Nicaraguan national interest but to anyone who opposed the Somoza family. Communism thus began to gain positive attributes or at least lose some of the dangerous trappings with which it is usually identified. In his analysis of the intellectual foundations of the Nicaraguan Revolution, Donald Hodges argues it was Anastasio Somoza García's identification of Sandino as a Communist that actually opened the way for FSLN leader Carlos Fonseca and other younger opponents of the regime to recover Sandino's legacy:

> The first book Fonseca's study group tackled was in fact Somoza's biography of Sandino. Ironically, the dictator's effort to document Sandino's links to the Mexican Communist party was the best argument he could have given for rescuing Sandino's legacy. By presenting evidence of Sandino's "bolshevism," Somoza's book strongly recommended itself to the youth of the PSN [Nicaraguan Socialist party] interested in the history of their country. By emphasizing the subversive content of Sandino's political philosophy and his efforts to make a communist revolution in Nicaragua up until the day he was assassinated, Somoza made Sandino appear reprehensible to respectable readers, but made him a hero to Fonseca's group.[19]

The ideology of the prerevolutionary regime itself deepened the crack in Somoza's edifice, as it had in Iran. However, a much more detailed analysis is needed to explain exactly how Islamic activism and Sandinismo became voices for *all* the Iranian and Nicaraguan people (at least for a historical moment).

The Ascent of Islamic Activism in Iran

In several scholarly works, it has been noted Shi'ism has especially salient features that pose a potential threat to state authority.[20] The Shi'ite Doctrine of Imamate, for instance, ascribes legitimate rule to the imams who were descendants of Ali, the successor of the prophet and the first Shi'ite imam. Since the occultation of the last imam in the ninth century, however, legitimate authority in the Shi'ite community has been in the hands of the ulama who, as representatives of the will of the imam, claimed the right to guide the community of believers.[21] Since the Shi'ites presumably do not differentiate between political and religious spheres, a tension has always existed between religious authority and political power. Stories abound about the struggles staged by various imams in resisting usurping temporal rulers.[22] One such story is especially heart-rending. It involves the third imam, Hosain, who bravely faced martyrdom in his attempt to institute the true, just Islamic society. This incident is used in religious preachments, especially during the month of Muharram when the incident is celebrated, to hold the Shi'ite community responsible for not helping the imam institute the just Islamic society.[23]

Despite the tension existing between religious authority and political power in theory, however, the ulama have generally cooperated with the rulers and legitimized their power throughout the course of Iranian history. That is, in practice, they have accepted the existence of temporal power and limited their leadership to the religious sphere. The political and anti-imperialist role of the clergy emerging at the end of the Qajar period, therefore, has not been treated by most scholars as a political development logically deduced from Shi'ite doctrines. Rather, the rift between the ulama and the Qajar state has been interpreted as a nationalist response to Western influence and the increasing incorporation of Iran into Western political and economic structures.[24] The rift later was also based on the threats posed to the religious leadership by a secular state that used military-bureaucratic reorganization to institute administrative, legal, economic, and educational reforms based on Western ideas — all of which were intended to enhance the power of the state vis-à-vis groups in civil society.

The development of an activist posture by the ulama did not mean a unified or consistent oppositional stance toward the state, even when the religious establishment was severely attacked by the state (e.g., during Reza Shah's reign). Two aspects of the state-ulama relationship can help explain this. First, the lack of a single, unified, and disciplined hierarchy, and the ties developed between some leading members of the religious establishment and the state, created schisms within the religious community with respect to the institution of monarchy. For instance, in his detailed analysis of state-ulama relations, Shahrough Akhavi reports on the various positions—ranging from active support to rejection—taken by the leading clergy during the nationalist period in the 1950s and the 1963 uprising.[25] Second, when the ulama's prerogatives have been effectively and suddenly attacked, as they were under Reza Shah, the religious community has found it difficult to gather resources and prepare to counterattack.[26]

This brief elaboration on the history of the ulama-state relationship immediately raises an important question. What were the added factors that propelled the ulama not only to oppose the monarchy but also to aspire to control the state? Three factors seem particularly important: (1) reemergence of Islamic nationalism, (2) development of an ideological basis for controlling the state, and (3) organizational prowess of the clergy. In the following pages, I lay out these factors and argue that some of them had been present throughout the twentieth century but became intensified during the prerevolutionary period, while others were new and related to the particular form the state-ulama relationship took during Mohammad Reza Shah's reign.

Reemergence of Islamic Nationalism

As mentioned earlier, the development of Shi'ism into a form of nationalism expressed in terms of the dominant cultural form went back to the advent of Western penetration. Hossein Bashiriyeh best explains this development:

> The increasing competition of foreign interests undermined the traditional petty commodity production centered in the bazaars. As a result the traditional petty bourgeoisie emerged as the social basis of resistance to western economic, political and cultural influence as the stronghold of nationalism. . . . It was from this conjuncture of interactions between Iranian and Western economies that early Iranian nationalism emerged as a protest movement. It was also the nature of this conjuncture that gave Iranian nationalism its particular characteristics: nationalism was expressed in terms of Islam and Islam was expressed in terms of nationalism.[27]

In the more recent period, this form of nationalism once again reappeared as the economic and sociopolitical position of the petty bourgeoisie of the bazaar, which had historically been the social basis of indigenous Islamic nationalism, began to deteriorate. The most persistent articulator of this rejuvenated nationalism was, of course, Ayatollah Ruhollah Khomeini, who from exile preached against "the ever increasing blows against Islam, the enserfment of the nation by the imperialists and their control of the bazaars and all military, political and commercial aspects of life."[28]

Khomeini was undoubtedly the hero of the bazaar petty bourgeoisie, but this rejuvenated Islamic nationalism was much more broad-based.[29] By the 1970s, it also attracted the young intelligentsia who had become concerned about Western cultural domination. This was an important development because this social grouping had traditionally shown affinities with secular ideologies. However, the need to separate themselves from anything Western made these ideologies—also identified with the West— less appealing. Furthermore, as mentioned above, since "nationalism with a pre-Islamic emphasis had been largely coopted by the Shah, the only competing ideology with the hope of mass support was some version of Shi'i Islam."[30] With the deepening revolutionary crisis, even the professional intermediate class, a class fairly inculcated with Western values, relented and accepted the Islamic leadership. By this time, as Said

Arjomand points out, Khomeini was seen as the embodiment of Iranian tradition, totally uncontaminated by the cultural alienation wrought by Western tradition.[31]

The appeal of the works of Ali Shariati, the popular lay ideologist, is just one example of the yearning for a "pure" national identity.[32] Although partly anticlerical, Shariati sought to restore the political role of religion and lay the theoretical foundation for a new Islamic political community. This new Islamic political community was derived from the active rejection of the West and an emphasis on the local economy and culture. By advocating "active" rejection, Shariati was attempting to do away with the traditional notion that one must passively wait for the end of the era of occultation until a just, Islamic government could be established. Because of this, he became very popular among the urban educated youth, predominantly from bazaari background. He was especially appreciated by such radical Islamic organizations as the Mojahedin-e Khalq, whose political agenda was based on a radical interpretation of Islam with a very strong anticapitalist and anti-imperialist bent.

Development of the Ideological Basis for Control of the State

On a more fundamental level, the essence of Shariati's thought hinted at the development of a new approach to the question of political authority. The schism between political and religious authorities that had characterized the Iranian community was no longer deemed satisfactory. The combination of this and the activist posture he advocated clearly called for an attack on the state and its reshaping according to Islamic principles. Shariati, however, was not very clear about how the Islamic ethos of his imagined community was going to reshape social, political, and legal institutions.[33] A much more coherent approach to the post-revolutionary state was developed by Khomeini, who coined the saying that ulama should rule directly in behalf of the hidden imam.

The idea that ulama should rule directly and its accompanying corollary that monarchy was illegitimate in Islam were indeed very radical within Shi'ism. These ideas negated both the quietism of the first centuries after the occultation and the parliamentary constitutional view that was predominant among the clerical reformers. As Willem Floor has indicated, in the twentieth century most ulama, particularly the higher ones, have been more conservative than revolutionary in their opposition; they wished to stop Western penetration and influence, not to create a new system of rule and society.[34] The cardinal question, therefore, is related to circumstances that led to the ascent of this radical position within the religious community.

Unfortunately, while many scholars have been quick to point out the emergence of this radical position, they have not been as successful in positing an adequate explanation for this change. Answers emphasizing the intensity of socioeconomic transformations can explain protests against the regime, but they cannot explain the noted change in the nature of these protests. The only satisfactory answer, to my mind, has been put forth by Hamid Enayat, who argues that the answer must be found in the processes and outcomes of the state-ulama struggles from the end of nineteenth century.[35] He specifically points to four episodes instrumental in bringing about a political transformation within Shi'ism: the "Tobacco Rebellion" of 1892, the Constitutional Revolution of 1906–11, the oil nationalization movement of 1951–53, and the abortive uprising of 1963 led by Khomeini. These episodes had similar processes, he argues, in that they all required an alliance among the main social and political forces in the country (the ulama, the indigenous propertied class, and secular nationalists), and they all depended on the active encouragement of the religious leaders to mobilize the masses.

With the exception of the 1963 uprising,[36] these events also had similar outcomes:

> On each occasion, while the religious leaders emerged as *immediate* bene-ficiaries, on each occasion, too, either the government or the semi-secular nationalists soon managed to gain the upper hand, and excluded their religious partners from power. . . . Accordingly, the Ulama genuinely drew three lessons from these: (i) whenever they campaign, there is nothing which can stand in their way of immediate success; (ii) in order to ensure the consummation of their success, they should not trust or share power with their secular or semi-secular rivals; (iii) the defeat of 1963 showed that religious leadership cannot have any hope of initial success unless it man-ages to have a degree of internal unity.[37]

The previous political experience, therefore, set the stage for a reevaluation of the goals of the religious movement and opened the way for the ascent of the radical position. Mastery over the popular move-ment was no longer deemed sufficient; the new resolve was to prevent others from usurping the fruits of religious efforts, namely state power.[38]

Organizational Prowess

If ideological maturation made the militant wing of the religious movement determined not to allow itself to be outwitted by the assort-ment of secular forces, it was their organizational capabilities that made popular mobilization and continued mastery over the popular movement possible. The Iranian religious community has always had certain economic and political resources that have given the ulama the organizational independence to react against state encroachments. Economic resources have included control over charitable/religious endowments (*awgaf*) given to institutions like schools, mosques, shrines, and hospitals. The ulama have also kept direct control over certain religious taxes, the so-called *khums* (one-fifth of agricultural and commercial profits) and *zakat* (levied on various categories of wealth and spent on purposes specified in the Quran), and the voluntary payments, *sadaga* (spent for purposes of charity) and *nuzur* (made for vows). According to Keddie, "The Ulama were able to use a combination of moral and physical pressure to collect, especially from the merchants and other well-off bazaar traders and artisans, the khums."[39] Furthermore, Keddie goes on to say that, while most of this was supposed to go to welfare and charity, a large sum contributed to a significant net increase in the wealth and power of the religious classes.[40] Finally, the most important political resource was the fact that the ulama's leadership resided in the Shi'i shrine cities in Iraq and was not controlled by Iran's government.

In short, the political and economic independence of the Shi'i bureaucracy was essential in the ulama's activism. It is important not to carry this point too far, however. Independent financial bases did not always lead to financial security or independent political activities. As Hamid Algar reports on the conditions during the Qajar dynasty, control of much of *awgaf* property was in the hands of the state, and "the yearly grants made to the Ulama ... could on occasion be intended as silence money."[41] In addition, dependence on individual contributions tended to make the ulama susceptible to the pressures of public opinion. The existence of these weaknesses allowed Reza Shah to attack religious institutions as ferociously as possible without instigating massive resistance.

After Reza Shah's abdication, however, there was a gradual rebuilding of clerical power and organization that can help explain clerical success in 1979. It is important to lay out these changes since they occurred in a round-about way, despite continued governmental attacks on some clerical prerogatives. The first change was the evolution of an efficient system, centered in the city of Qum, for the collection and distribution of religious taxes and alms.[42] This system was developed by Ayatollah Hajj Hossein Borujerdi, the sole "source of imitation" between 1947 and 1961, at a time when the religious leadership was encouraging political quietism. It created a sounder financial basis for the religious community and a network of communication linked directly to Qum, which were later used by Islamic militants to foster a more activist orientation.

The second change was the emergence of a new religious stratum. As mentioned, in the past, the ulama were largely dependent on the populace for their financial resources, although some were under the state's direct pay. The expansion of the state and the availability of more varied resources, however, gave rise to a new stratum that was relatively independent from both public donations and direct state support. Enayat best explains this phenomenon and its consequences for the religious community:

> Thanks to a variety of fresh job opportunities—teaching in non-religious institutions, schools and universities, journalism, publishing, etc.—they were able to earn enough to be independent of both the patriarchal Ulama and the state if they wanted to—although in terms of religious dogma they were inevitably affiliated to one or the other of the Ulama. This brought them nearer to other groups of educated people—teachers, lectures, writers and intellectuals in general—with all that is meant in terms of exposure to radicalizing currents, and response to social and political strains. Much of, but by no means all, the ideological and organizational work which consciously or unconsciously prepared the ground for the religious leadership of the Revolution, especially the political use of the mosques, was done by this group.[43]

It was this group that created the necessary ideological bridge between the religious community and the rest of the society. More important, this group, by incorporating ideas developed by theorists like Shariati, pushed the religious community as a whole toward militancy.

The Emergence of a Christian-Marxist Dialogue in Nicaragua

The ideas that became identified with the Nicaraguan Revolution, like their Iranian counterparts, had their roots in the history of a nation continuously striving to rid itself of foreign domination and internal despotism. They drew heavily from the memory of struggles against these evils in Nicaragua and similar struggles in other peripheral formations. The origins of these memories were diverse, reflecting the multiplicity of opposition to Somoza's antidemocratic, antinationalist, and anticommunist regime. One of the fascinating aspects of the Nicaraguan Revolution is how these diverse ideological currents eventually came together under the hegemony of Sandinismo. The story of how this happened reveals the ideological dynamics of the Nicaraguan Revolution as well as what Sandinismo ultimately turned out to be. To tell the story, I begin with the FSLN and then move on to discuss its encounter with other ideological currents in the hope of unraveling the reasons for the ideological ascent of Sandinismo as well as its mutations.

From its founding in the early 1960s, the FSLN attempted to forge a link between the contemporary struggle by Marxist-Leninists, who had come under the influence of the Cuban Revolution, and Augusto Sandino's struggle against imperialism and dictatorship. Drawing from the Cuban Revolution, founding members of the FSLN, like Carlos Fonseca, insisted on not only adapting Marxism to the peculiar conditions of their country but also remolding it as part of an indigenous movement independent of the local Communist party. As Hodges points out, "What Fidel Castro's revival of José Martí did for the July 26 movement in Cuba, Fonseca's recovery of Sandino's political legacy did for the struggle against imperialism and dictatorship in Nicaragua."[44] The adaptation of Sandino's ideas and example served a political and tactical function.

Politically, it separated the FSLN from the strictly Marxist-Leninist project of the Nicaraguan Socialist party (PSN) since the latter vehemently rejected the FSLN's concessions to popular ideology. Constrained by the conservatism of its Soviet-bloc backers, the PSN regarded the Nicaraguan masses as backward and not ready for revolution. It remained committed in theory and practice to revolution only after the maturation of social conditions and the organization of the proletariat. The FSLN's rejection of this position proved both necessary and helpful on two grounds. First, since Marxism-Leninism in Nicaragua constantly faced the regime's anticommunism, an ideology that did not use the same imagery and at times even contradicted some of its premises turned out to be more successful in mobilizing people. Second, in rejecting the PSN's supervision, the Sandinistas were able to develop a project with aspirations for immediate state power. After all, if the Cubans could do it, so could the Nicaraguans.

Tactically, the figure of the heroic general standing against insurmountable odds was indispensable in mobilizing the masses for a general insurrection. Sandino's resistance was also an important source of inspiration for the guerrilla strategy, which although not very successful, kept the FSLN on the Nicaraguan political map despite the regime's systematic and vicious campaigns against it. To be sure, the FSLN's survival continuously required a reevaluation of tactics and strategies. Ultimately, however, Sandino's tactical influence, as well as the FSLN's costly defeats at the hands of the regime, moved the organization away from viewing armed struggle as the only road to power. Instead, the FSLN began emphasizing that the key to overthrowing the regime lay in the guerrillas' mobilizing the local populace through well-planned political and organizational activity. It was through these interactions that revolutionary ideas began to take shape. As was partially discussed in the last chapter, the most important component of this interaction was the development of a Marxist-Christian dialogue and cooperation that ultimately proved explosive within the Nicaraguan context. I have just laid out the manner through which Marxism become more flexible and receptive in Nicaragua, but it is also important to discuss the road Christianity took before fully committing itself to Sandinista leadership in the overthrow of the Somoza regime.

Like that of Marxism, the history of Catholicism in Nicaragua must begin with the larger environment within which it operated. Historically, the weight of Catholic influence in Nicaragua, as in the rest of Latin America, has gone to reinforce existing social arrangements. This does not mean there were no tensions between religious and political authorities. But, traditionally, the problems religion posed to the political order were in terms of "church-state conflicts, centering over the control of schools, the regulation of marriage and divorce, birth control, and the like."[45] The increasing penetration of capitalism and the rise of antichurch, liberal governments at the turn of the century, however, forced the Latin American church to begin to come to terms with the new political and economic order.

Initially, it sought to strengthen its traditional ties with conservative political groups, but its emphasis moved, especially after World War II, to evangelization and social reform.[46] Accordingly, laypeople were motivated to begin reasserting the church's influence through the formation of political parties and labor unions. The church also began to establish a significant presence among the poor in the cities and rural areas. This process of leaving their relatively well-off parishes to tend to the needs of their poorer flock ultimately proved a radicalizing experience for many members of the Catholic church. Andrew Bradstock best explains how this happened:

> The church's encounter with the peasants (or *compesinos*) stimulated a dialectical learning process known as *Concientizacion* in which, by working alongside the poor, the missionaries came to understand more deeply their situation and, in turn, endeavoured to bring them to an understanding of their conditions and the possibilities for change. Drawing heavily from the teaching of the Brazilian educationist Paulo Freire they sought to demythologize the social order and encourage an awareness in the people that their poverty was not divinely ordained but rooted in the prevailing political and economic arrangements which, being human creations, could be subject to change.[47]

In other words, a process that began with the intention of helping the poor deal with their changing environment turned into, at least among some parts of the church, a rejection of the injustice present in the structures of the society and a commitment to liberation from those injustices. This change of attitude was even partially articulated in the Medellín document, which came out of the Second General Conference of Latin American Bishops. According to Bradstock, the change manifested itself by the different methodology adopted at Medellín, which no longer "spoke in general terms of progress and transformation in an apparently neutral ideological framework." Instead, it emphasized the analysis of the concrete situations encountered. The result was an endorsement of "pastoral work already in progress on the ground."[48]

Many perceived this shift away from an "academic" to a "praxis-centered" theology as a move toward a theology that encouraged the interpretation of the biblical texts in the light of an active commitment to liberation. This even opened the way for the possibility of using non-Christian texts (including Marxist) to suggest "how the goal of the kingdom of God may be built within history."[49] More important, it was the active commitment to liberation that allowed the expansion of the concept of sin to include not only private moral behavior but also societal injustices and introduced aspirations for a "classless" society into Christian theology.[50]

In Nicaragua, the process was shaping up as early as the 1960s. To be sure, the church hierarchy continued to remain silent. But for some Christians, revolutionary commitment followed community dialogues and Bible studies. This was especially because, faced with a shortage of priests to carry out the task of improving the condition of the poor, the church offered basic training to laypeople, who became known as Delegates of the Word and returned to their own communities with a socially oriented gospel.[51] This combination of religious training and detailed knowledge of community problems proved explosive among these lay Christians. Even the higher levels of the church hierarchy were left with no other option except opposition when faced with Somoza's excesses after the 1972 earthquake. By the time the church hierarchy decided to give its unequivocal sign of support for the revolution, however, it was the voice of dialogues in the Christian base communities that had become incorporated into the voice of insurrection.[52] In his study of Solentiname,[53] the most celebrated Christian base community engaged in raising revolutionary consciousness, Phillip Berryman discusses the basic dynamic that moved all such communities in Nicaragua:

> The pastoral agent brings a knowledge of the scripture, and the people bring their experience of life—and both learn from each other. However, it is not simply a Scriptures-and-life division of labor, since the pastoral agents usually have to encourage the people by showing appreciation for

their culture and indeed for their ability to think and express themselves. Thus the people themselves often find new pearls in the Scripture texts, despite the fact that they have hitherto usually been led to believe that those "above" (authorities, politicians, priests, teachers, doctors) have *the* word. . . . In the basic-Christian community process, both members and leaders acquire a "key" to the Scriptures, a basic approach that helps them to understand fundamental concepts and to make connection between the Scriptures and their lives. Underlying it all seems to be a basic change in attitude from one of accepting the world as it is to one aiming at transforming it—becoming active agents or subjects of history, as is frequently said in Spanish. This involves a change in religious vision from one in which God made things the way they are—us poor and others rich—to one in which God calls us to assume responsibility. Certain values become central: human dignity, basic human equality (as an underlying fact and as something to be worked out), unity, struggle, hope.[54]

The centrality of these values gives us clues about how this radical Christian vision became fused with FSLN ideas to create the ideology of insurrection. These values also represented the core of Sandinista ideology.[55] What is important, however, is that their representation in Christian form made it easier for the public to understand the Sandinista message. This does not mean Christian theology was merely a tool the Sandinistas used to attract support for the insurrection. The fusion was much more complex. The Christian base communities were attracted to the FSLN's message, but in their dialogue with it they also left their mark. For instance, the Marxist-Christian dialogue profoundly influenced the conception of the new human beings shaped by the revolution. As Hodges points out, the new human being not only was personified in people like Che Guevarra but also was publicly equated with Jesus Christ, still the most revered example of love and sacrifice among the Christian poor.[56] "For the bulk of the FSLN's Christian followers, the formation of a new person depended on faith in the Christian revelation of Jesus as the Son of God, in conjunction with the Old Testament belief that man is created in God's image."[57] This image of the new person was very different from the image of an inaccessible (but kindhearted) party vanguard giving knowledge and "correct" direction to malleable masses. By introducing this imagery to the Nicaraguan revolutionary discourse, the Christian supporters at least introduced an ideological tool with which the vanguard tendencies could be kept in check.

Summing Up

The discussion of ideological mobilization in this chapter was intended to shed light on the process through which certain ideas or slogans came to represent the struggle against the old regimes in Iran and Nicaragua. This does not mean that other ideas or slogans did not exist. Rather, my point is that the process through which a particular view of the world comes to dominate revolutionary rhetoric is important for understanding the boundaries within which the "new" social reality is created. Revolutions are not purely destructive events. They are also creative insofar as they allow individuals and groups to articulate and pursue different visions of the past and the future. In this chapter, I argued the success, at least for a historical moment, of a particular vision was dependent on the ideological structure of the old regime as well as ideological, political, and organizational mutations that occurred within the opposition forces. Hence, in Iran, the official anti-Islamic nationalism of the shah's regime made suspect other Western-derived forms of expression, while changes within the Islamic community opened the way for the ascent of radical forces. In Nicaragua, Somoza's attempts to buttress his regime through the use of democratic trappings helped to delegitimize reformist politics pursued by the bourgeoisie, while changes within the Marxist and Christian opposition created the conditions for a powerful dialogue that ultimately undermined the regime. This does not mean ideological mobilization against the Iranian and Nicaraguan regimes alone can explain the outbreak and processes of these revolutions; it simply means it is an important explanatory factor, together with the other factors laid out in previous chapters. Similarly, ideology cannot explain revolutionary outcome by itself. As will be demonstrated in the next chapter, the boundaries within which revolutionary rhetoric emerges during the revolutionary process also powerfully shape revolutionary outcome.

NOTES

1. It is important to distinguish between ideological mass mobilization for change and the role played by ideology in defending and consolidating a victorious revolution. As will be shown in the next chapter, ideology in the construction of a new society becomes much more articulated and organized.

2. G. Therborn, *The Ideology of Power and the Power of Ideology* (London: New Left Books, 1980), p. 2. In conceptualizing the operation of ideology in terms of the formation of human subjectivity, Therborn is clearly influenced by Louis Althusser's seminal piece "Ideology and Ideological State Apparatuses," in *Lenin and Philosophy and Other Essays* (New York: Monthly Review Press, 1971), pp. 127–93.

3. A. Swidler, "Culture in Action: Symbols and Strategies," *American Sociological Review* 51 (April 1986), pp. 273–86.

4. Ibid., p. 279.

5. Therborn, *The Ideology of Power*, p. 17. This conception of ideology differs from the traditional Marxist approach, which sees ideology as forms of consciousness either corresponding to class interest ("true" consciousness) or not ("false" consciousness), and from the liberal conception (followed by Skocpol), which sees it as bodies of thought that we possess and invest in our actions.

6. Ibid., pp. 120–21.

7. In using the notion of dangerous memory of conflict and exclusion in the process of ideological mobilization, I have drawn heavily from S. H. Welsh, *Communities of Resistance and Solidarity: A Feminist Theology of Liberation* (New York: Orbis, 1985), chapter 3. Welsh uses this notion in relation to liberation theology. I have found it useful in understanding the general process of ideological mobilization as well.

8. Ibid., p. 36.

9. Ibid., p. 42.

10. Ibid., p. 119–20.

11. My use of this term is influenced by Benedict Anderson's brilliant study of nationalism, *Imagined Community* (London: Verso, 1983). Anderson borrows the term from Seton-Watson and applies it mostly to European nationalism after the 1820s.

12. F. Halliday, *Iran: Dictatorship and Development* (New York: Penguin, 1979), pp. 140–46.

13. For much of what follows in this section, I am indebted to N. R. Keddie's chapter on modern Iranian political thought in *Roots of Revolution: An Interpretive History of Modern Iran* (New Haven, Conn.: Yale University Press, 1981), pp. 183–202.

14. Ibid., p. 191–92.

15. Ibid., p. 192.

16. One of his most commonly used life-sized portraits showed him emerging from the clouds and extending his hand toward the onlookers, who were presumably the people in the shah-people equation.

17. H. Weber, *Nicaragua: The Sandinist Revolution* (London: New Left Books, 1981), p. 19.

18. Ibid.

19. D. C. Hodges, *Intellectual Foundations of the Nicaraguan Revolution* (Austin: University of Texas Press, 1986), pp. 163–64.

20. See, for instance, H. Algar, *Religion and State in Iran: 1785–1906* (Berkeley: University of California Press, 1969), and N. R. Keddie, "The Roots of Ulama's Power in Modern Iran," in *Scholars, Saints and Sufis*, ed. N. R. Keddie (Berkeley: University of California Press, 1972), pp. 211–29.

21. Obviously, this is a very sketchy elaboration on a very complex set of ideas. For instance, the role of ulama is complicated by the fact that only years of religious study give some of the clerics the possibility of interpreting imam's will.

But, unlike the imam, they remain fallible. The purpose here, however, is to give a general sense of the Shi'ite world view. The revolution in Iran has brought forth a large number of excellent works on religion in Iran. See, for instance, S. Akhavi, *Religion and Politics in Contemporary Iran* (Albany: State University of New York Press, 1980); S. A. Arjomand, *The Shadow of God and the Hidden Imam* (Chicago: University of Chicago Press, 1984); and M. J. Fischer, *Iran: From Religious Dispute to Revolution* (Cambridge, Mass.: Harvard University Press, 1980).

22. Fischer, *Iran*, pp. 12–27.

23. Ibid., p. 21.

24. See Algar, *Religion and State in Iran*, and N. R. Keddie, "Origins of Religious-Radical Alliances," *Past and Present*, no. 34 (July 1966), pp. 70–86.

25. Akhavi, *Religion and Politics in Contemporary Iran*.

26. Reza Shah's attacks on the religious establishment were much more vicious and sudden than the attack initiated by his son. Reza Shah created a nationwide, secular public educational system at all levels, Western-influenced legal codes, and state-run welfare institutions that undermined the ulama's control of legal, educational, and welfare institutions. In addition, he forcefully imposed Western dress on both the clergy and women. For the list of attacks, see ibid.

27. H. Bashiriyeh, *State and Revolution in Iran, 1962–1982* (New York: St. Martin's Press, 1984), pp. 53–54.

28. Quoted in ibid., p. 61.

29. As Keddie points out, this is indeed the paradox of the Iranian situation: Islam came to play an even greater role in the Iranian opposition movement, "even though the number and power of Westernized secularized Iranians had grown greatly." N. R. Keddie, "Comments on Skocpol," *Theory and Society* 11 (May 1982), p. 290.

30. Ibid. This is not to suggest that Western-originated idea systems like Marxism were not present but simply to explain the popular appeal of Shi'i Islam.

31. S. A. Arjomand, *The Turban for the Crown* (New York: Oxford University Press, 1988), p. 109.

32. Another important figure was Jalal Al-e Ahmad, who was originally affiliated with the Tudeh party but increasingly developed an appreciation of Islam as a means of ideological mobilization. His main theme, however, was objection to Western economic, political, and cultural infiltration. See B. Hanson, "The Westoxication of Iran: Depictions and Reactions of Behrangi, Al-e Ahmad, and Shariati," *International Journal of Middle East Studies* 15, 1 (1983), pp. 1–23.

33. On ambiguities in Shariati's works, see S. Akhavi, "Shariati's Social Thought," in *Religion and Politics in Iran*, ed. N. R. Keddie (New Haven, Conn.: Yale University Press, 1983), pp. 125–44.

34. W. M. Floor, "The Revolutionary Character of the Iranian Ulama: Wishful Thinking or Reality?" *International Journal of Middle East Studies* 12, 4 (1980), pp. 501–24.

35. H. Enayat, "Revolution in Iran 1979: Religion as Political Ideology," in *Revolutionary Theory and Political Reality*, ed. Noel O'Sullivan (New York: St. Martin's Press, 1983), pp. 197–200.

36. The 1963 uprising, which ended in a crushing defeat of the ulama, was characterized by a rift within the religious community. The intransigent, anti-royalist stand of Khomeini created a gulf between him and the more conservative ulama.

37. Enayat, "Revolution in Iran," pp. 198–99.

38. The following quote, cited by Enayat, from the leading Islamic thinker Morteza Mottaheri, is perhaps the best indication of this sentiment: "The history of Islamic movements during the last hundred years reveals one unfortunate defect in its leadership: it has continued the struggle under its leadership [only] up to the moment of victory, but has refused to carry it on further [preferring instead] to go after its own business and allow others to usurp the results of its efforts." Ibid., p. 199.

39. Keddie, *Roots of Revolution*, p. 17.

40. These collections were used to support poor religious students, who formed the immediate constituency of each of the ulama (sometimes acting as their private armies), and employees of religious welfare institutions.

41. Algar, *Religion and State in Iran*, p. 16.

42. According to Algar, bookkeeping was introduced to account for the receipt and dispersion of donations, and "a register" was established of local agents authorized to collect money and forward it to Qum. H. Algar, "The Oppositional Role of the Ulama in Twentieth Century Iran," in *Scholars, Saints, and Sufis*, ed. N. R. Keddie (Berkeley: University of California Press, 1972), p. 243.

43. Enayat, "Revolution in Iran," pp. 203–4.

44. Hodges, *Intellectual Foundations of the Nicaraguan Revolution*, p. 193.

45. D. H. Levine, "Religion and Politics, Politics and Religion: An Introduction," in *Church and Politics in Latin America*, ed. D. H. Levine (Beverly Hills, Calif.: Sage, 1979), pp. 19–20.

46. For a short history of the church in Latin American, see A. Bradstock, *Saints and Sandinistas* (London: Epworth Press, 1987), chapter 1.

47. Ibid., p. 4.

48. Ibid., p. 8.

49. Ibid., p. 7.

50. According to Lancaster, liberation theology, like traditional Christianity, defines sin as that which estranges the individual from God. Liberation theology, however, underlines and develops the point by collapsing the distinction between the social and the spiritual. From this point of view, estrangement from God is measured in terms of our estrangement from the community. That which most radically divides people and estranges humanity from God is exploitation. Sin originates in the deliberate actions of those who pursue wealth and in the process of their accumulating wealth. If those ravaged by this process (the poor) respond to it with despair, then they have internalized sin and lost

faith. In liberation theology, "God redeems the poor through a process that is indissolubly linked to social vision and social action. . . . Revolution thus redeems the poor by sweeping aside despair . . . it moves the community [of believers] closer to God by diminishing the realm of exploitation that constitutes sin and estrangement." R. N. Lancaster, *Thanks to God and Revolution: Popular Religion and Class Consciousness in the New Nicaragua* (New York: Columbia University Press, 1988), pp. 76–79.

51. G. Ruchwarger, *People in Power* (South Hadley, Mass.: Bergin & Garvey, 1987), p. 39.

52. As will be discussed in the next chapter, the distinction between the church hierarchy and the Christian base communities is an important one since the hierarchy's support for the FSLN did not prove as solid as the support of the religious communities.

53. Solentiname was a Christian base community started by Ernesto Cardenal, a priest and poet, and later Nicaragua's minister of culture. The dialogues that occurred in Solentiname attract attention because they were preserved in a series of gospel discussions recorded during 1971–76, transcribed, and lightly edited by Cardenal. In this sense, Solentiname was not a typical Christian base community, since the more typical ones had lay (peasant) leadership. Observers, however, agree that discussions in Solentiname were surprisingly similar in both style and content to dialogues in more ordinary circumstances. On this issue and a more extensive discussion of Solentiname, see P. Berryman, *The Religious Roots of Rebellion* (New York: Orbis, 1984).

54. Ibid., p. 22.

55. Or, in Lancaster's words, "if the atmosphere of socialist revolution is most intensely an atmosphere of religious revivalism, it is because the Nicaraguan revolution has delivered socialism out of the womb of Christianity." Lancaster, *Thanks to God and Revolution,* p. 79.

56. Hodges, *Intellectual Foundations of the Nicaraguan Revolution,* p. 261.

57. Ibid., p. 263.

5

Revolutionary Outcomes

Can wine distilled from poison escape being poisonous? Can art
distilled in an era of evil escape being pernicious? Can politics
created out of an era of evil escape its evil tactics?

  —M. J. Fischer's rendition of Sadeq Hedayat's
  The Blind Owl in "Repetitions in the Iranian
  Revolution"

To discuss the outcome of recent revolutions is a chancy exercise.
Much of the problem lies with the term *outcome*, which connotes an
observable and fixed result, when the revolutionary process is still unfolding. The historical proximity of the Iranian and Nicaraguan revolutions clearly does not afford the long-term hindsight needed to unravel
their general characters. Yet there are certain similarities and differences
that are observable even now. Revolutionary regimes in both countries,
despite challenges, consolidated power effectively and oversaw the development of more bureaucratized states quite capable of maintaining the
mobilization of relatively large sectors of the population.[1] Both regimes
also were able to carry out at least some of their programs, despite the
burden of major wars that caused thousands of casualties in Nicaragua
and hundreds of thousands in Iran and resulted in billions of dollars of
property damage. At the same time, both countries suffered serious
economic crises, generated by the hostile international environment
surrounding them and the inability of the revolutionary leadership to
resolve intense class conflicts unleashed by the revolutionary processes.
These important similarities, however, should not overshadow differences
in terms of actual policies followed and the manner through which each
of these regimes became stabilized.

The Islamic revolutionaries have been the most successful in the
political and cultural arenas. A theocratic state intent on remolding
people's "ways of life" has been instituted, and the results of this generalized commitment to Islamic principles have been unambiguous. The

monarchy was abolished, and the elite directly associated with it was displaced. The administrative, judicial, and coercive apparatuses was reorganized and used for vicious attacks on the life-styles and institutional supports of social groupings with supposed links to the West as well as those opposed to the regime for any reason.[2] The Islamic leadership executed not only former members of the shah's army and the secret police but also many who participated in the shah's overthrow—members of moderate and leftist parties, ethnic minorities, and intellectuals, among others. The regime also was quick to respond to political forces representing the working class and the peasantry. Any independent attempt to organize on the part of the workers was regarded as a threat to the newly formed state. Accordingly, the formal wages of workers were cut, the oppositional workers councils (shuras) and individual workers were purged, and force and repression were used extensively to undercut worker militancy.[3] The regime's response to peasant militancy was similar. It either opposed land seizures or tended to ignore the plight of poor peasants.[4]

This brutal and successful neutralization or elimination of all opposition groups was done without destroying the repressive apparatus connected to the old regime.[5] To be sure, changes were made to assure control of the state apparatus, but these changes were mostly limited to decapitation as the prerevolutionary leaders were replaced by loyalists. Even the old imperial army was maintained. In fact, although it was weakened when its leadership was liquidated, the traditional military apparatus was slowly rehabilitated by the war with Iraq. Of course, the Islamic state-builders were able to further the powers of the state over society by adding a mass-incorporating element. Unlike the previous leaders, they were able to incorporate some of the popular energy unleashed during the revolution in auxiliary organizations, like the Revolutionary Guards.[6] This combination of state power from the previous regime and popular energy from the current one allowed total consolidation of power in less than two years.

But this success did not even begin to resolve the underlying political problems that were articulated during the revolutionary period. It merely subdued them under a very strong fist. For instance, the population continues to lack elementary political freedoms and is subject to the same methods of surveillance and control that it was under the previous regime. The revolutionary leaders also continue the same, if not heavier-handed, pattern of political and administrative centralization that created serious grievances among various nationalities in Iran.

Neither was much done in the rural sector. The first land reform bill, which was approved in April 1980, did allow for sweeping land distribution to landless and land-poor peasants. This law limited land-owners who directly cultivated their land to three times the acreage deemed sufficient, in each district, to maintain one peasant family. Absentee landlords, with no other source of income, were limited to twice this amount. Opposition from landowners and leading Islamic jurists, however, led to the suspension of the articles dealing with expropriation of private property. The Council of Guardians, a clerical body which can veto parliamentary legislation, even blocked a much more conservative bill, requiring landlords merely to lease their land in excess of limits set by the parliament to the local peasants under sharecropping, rental, or partnership agreements, on the grounds that it violated Islamic and constitutional principles.

In general, despite successes in postrevolutionary state-building, the Islamic revolutionaries have not been able to devise, much less institute, an "Islamic" economic plan that would clearly differentiate them from their predecessors. In other words, no systematic effort to articulate, let alone implement, a comprehensive revolutionary program of economic and social reform has been made. In fact, the revolutionary leadership has approached the economy on an ad hoc basis. Agricultural output is still stagnant, the capacity of industrial production is underutilized, unemployment is rampant, and not even a literacy campaign has been promulgated.

To be sure, the government took several important steps. The banking system was nationalized and brought under the auspices of five specialized banking entities in the fields of commerce (two groups), agriculture, industries and mines, and housing and construction. Nationalization also affected three broad categories of industries: heavy industries, industries owned by individuals closely associated with the old regime, and industries in economic difficulty because their liabilities exceeded their net assets. But the application of these laws was often haphazard, and, more important, it mostly led to increased government encroachment in the economy rather than to a better distribution of wealth and economic opportunity.[7] In addition, the inability to institute serious reforms also meant continuing dependence on oil exports to the West and, hence, the inability to combat cyclical fluctuations that characterize the world capitalist system. According to a recent study, the Iranian oil strategy seems to be based on an uncoordinated policy that essentially targets high oil exports, prices, and revenues at any cost.[8]

The Nicaraguan revolutionaries also consolidated power but in a much less bloody manner, despite constant threats from the United States.[9] While debate went on about whether or not the 1984 elections were truly democratic, there is no doubt that Nicaragua had a degree of pluralism atypical of revolutionary societies. Instead of dismantling opposition through repression and force, the FSLN generally relied on parallel organizations to weaken existing organizations (ranging from newspapers to trade unions) that were not necessarily tied to the FSLN. The formation of the so-called popular church to offset the strength of the Catholic hierarchy is a perfect example of the government's attempt to undermine an established institution.[10] The use of political means also was quite successful in controlling opposition political parties. By neither excluding private-sector representatives from government nor allowing them to gain control of key political institutions (e.g., the military and mass organizations), the FSLN was able to establish a hegemonic position within the new political system without violently repressing the activities of other political parties.

The Nicaraguan revolutionaries also differed from their Iranian counterparts in their serious attempt to restructure the economy. This does not mean that the Sandinistas were able to create a healthy economic environment—quite the contrary. After an initial period of recovery (1979–82), Nicaragua's economy deteriorated. Soon Nicaragua was in the grips of severe economic crisis, with important industrial sectors in a state of collapse, uncontrollable inflation and foreign debt, and a large trade deficit.[11] Nevertheless, important changes were deliberately initiated within the economy. For instance, the new government wasted no time in setting up goals for reactivating the economy and reconstituting it as a mixed system—including both private and state enterprises—and redistributing income within the limitations of Nicaragua's economic possibilities. From the beginning, it is important to note, the revolutionary regime made no attempt to socialize the entire productive process or eliminate private capital. The attempt to enlist the cooperation of private enterprise was based on the premise that it was not possible to socialize all the means of production in an underdeveloped economy like Nicaragua's. Yet despite a commitment to a mixed economy, the revolution significantly altered the proportion of total GDP produced by the different forms of property.

Two important changes are worth mentioning. Not surprisingly, the revolution greatly increased the role of the state sector in the production of GDP (from 11 percent in 1977 to 39 percent in 1982). The other result was an increase in the share generated by the many small private producers and the growing number of cooperatives in the country (from 22 percent to 30 percent).[12] The combination of these two changes suggests a rather peculiar development: the uneven expansion of the state sector. This means that, while the state controlled over half of the "modern sector" GDP (commercial and banking sectors, construction, modern manufacturing, and estate agriculture), the state's share in gross material production was only one-quarter and in agricultural production was about one-fifth.[13] Peasant agriculture (producing foodstuffs) and the agricultural export sector (cotton, coffee, livestock, and sugar) mostly remained outside state ownership. As we will see in the next section, the roots of this development can be traced to the kind of ownership exercised by Somoza in the prerevolutionary economy.

Since agriculture was so important to the economy,[14] agrarian reform was the centerpiece of the revolution. Moreover, the Sandinistas showed quite a bit of flexibility and pragmatism in dealing with the land question. Originally, the process of agrarian reform led to the state's expropriating land belonging to Somoza and his associates and managing it as collective farms, organizing peasant producers into cooperatives, and providing strong incentives for large capitalist producers so they would keep on producing.[15] All this was done while peasant proprietors and largely private commercial farms retained an important role in the economy. Later, however, the Sandinistas shifted their approach. A massive amount of usable land was redistributed to the landless organized in production cooperatives, and support to peasant capitalists and small independent commercial producers, particularly those living in areas of military conflict, was increased.[16] Throughout this process, organizations representing those directly affected by governmental policies—peasants and rural workers—had an important influence in such areas as credit policy and, more important, "in assuring that peasants and landless [were] given the opportunity to choose whether they want to farm agrarian reform land collectively or as individual holdings."[17] The Sandinista policy of land reform increasingly moved in a more decentralized and pro-peasant direction because of the influence exerted by popular classes.

Understanding Revolutionary Outcome

This brief elaboration gives us an overview of conditions in Iran and Nicaragua, but how can the similarities and differences be explained? Following Skocpol, I argue against understanding outcomes as the result of actors attempting to implement a certain ideological vision of the ideal social order.[18] Instead, I utilize an approach that analyzes revolutionary outcomes in terms of the struggles surrounding the creation of new state organizations within the social revolutionary situation. Unlike Skocpol, however, in explaining the struggle over state control, I take the role of ideological structures and class interests seriously. Using this combination, I intend to demonstrate that the variation and similarities in revolutionary outcomes can be better understood by focusing on the political struggles to control and maintain state power within the constraints imposed, and the opportunities afforded, by the existing economic, political, and ideological structures, the international context, and the class relations of the revolution itself.[19]

Understanding revolutionary outcomes as fixed results powerfully shaped by idea systems deployed as self-conscious political arguments by political actors is rejected for a simple reason: one cannot make sense of revolutionary results by simply referring to the differences in the intentions or ideological pronouncements of individual or collective actors. While the Islamic revolutionaries and the Sandinistas used different symbolism and ideological referents, they (and for that matter, other revolutionaries in peripheral formations) articulated similar goals and desires. In the economic sphere, they called for types of production and distribution that were oriented toward meeting the basic needs of the majority of the population. In the political sphere, they called for the reconstitution of state-society relations so that the subordinated classes (popular classes in the Sandinista terminology, the downtrodden in the Iranian context) would have a higher degree of participation in determining public policy. Finally, discussions of economic distribution and political participation were situated within the context of struggle against U.S. imperialism at all levels (from economic to cultural).

Yet the Iranian and Nicaraguan revolutionaries clearly had different practices. For instance, as mentioned before, there is no doubt that the Sandinistas showed more tolerance for political pluralism and participatory democracy than their Iranian counterparts did. As I demonstrate in the following pages, part of the explanation for this difference can be found in the struggle to control and maintain state power. It cannot, for instance, be simply explained by the Sandinistas' socialist inclinations. As is well known, twentieth-century socialists have supported varying degrees of democracy or authoritarianism according to the sociopolitical context. But the socialist habit of institutionalizing authoritarian practices beyond the particular sociopolitical context in which they were evoked and then claiming that the new autocratic polity represents a higher form of political governance was not pursued in Nicaragua.

At the same time, the historical development of Sandinismo, first as an oppositional political culture and then as a state ideology, is not irrelevant either. As I suggested in the previous chapter, the pattern of ideological mass mobilization is always important for understanding the nature of revolutionary confrontation. Furthermore, with the victory of oppositional forces, and with its full-fledged articulation, revolutionary language takes on added importance because it sets the boundaries within which the revolutionaries operate. In Nicaragua, it was not what socialism had done elsewhere that mattered. Rather, choices made available through the Sandinista revolutionary rhetoric, itself connected to the Marxist-Christian dialogue discussed in the previous chapter, also determined the future of Nicaragua. It is by understanding revolutionary rhetoric as an instrument of political and social change that this study can claim to reconcile the role of revolutionaries as both ideologues and state-builders. We can agree with Skocpol that the revolutionaries' ideological vision is continuously undercut by the exigencies of the attempt to take and hold state power, but, at the same time, the existence of historically shaped visions cannot be denied. At least the extent of their strength must be investigated since, after a revolution, their articulation and autonomy crucially determine the fate of the mobilized population. The attempt to gain and hold state power may make the revolutionaries more "pragmatic" as they deal with the revolutionary crisis and the "carry-overs" from the old regime. But this pragmatism is always situated within the possibilities and impossibilities afforded by the process of ideological transformation.

A similar argument can be made in relation to the question of class interest. To be sure, Skocpol is correct in belittling the importance of class interest in favor of an emphasis on the political resources available to the would-be state-builders. As shown below, it is essential to see the Shi'ite clerics' and Sandinistas' rise to power in terms of the organizational structures that endowed them with the ability and desire to fill the power vacuum created by the paralysis and sudden collapse of the Iranian and Nicaraguan states in 1979. It is also correct to see their success in light of the politico-military mobilization of popular support in their wars against domestic counterrevolutionaries and competitors and against foreign invaders. This explanation, however, is not enough for understanding important peculiarities in both revolutions.

For instance, it cannot explain why, despite the vicious counterrevolutionary efforts of the U.S. government, the Sandinista leadership continued to dwell on the question of democracy in a serious manner.[20] To be sure, this costly undeclared war, like most foreign efforts to subvert emerging revolutionary regimes, helped the Sandinistas consolidate a mass-mobilizing, centralized regime through nationalist appeals and a heavy military buildup.[21] U.S. intervention also was used as a justification for many of the authoritarian practices of the Sandinistas. Nevertheless, the relative openness of the Sandinista regime is an important difference that an approach simply focused on the struggle for state power cannot explain. Neither can it explain why the ruling clerics in Iran consistently refused to attack private property, despite tremendous pressure within the religious community to do so.

For answers to these types of questions we need to look at the class configurations within civil society and the class links the revolutionaries developed during the period of revolutionary mobilization. The examination of these links will reveal, for instance, that the support the Islamic activists received from the merchants during the revolution played a very important role in preventing the government from instituting more distributive policies. In general, the examination of class links developed during the revolutionary period helps to highlight further the limitations state-builders face and the resources they are able to draw from in their attempt to transform society.

A final factor for understanding the outcomes in Iran and Nicaragua is the way these countries are situated in the world context. Iran and Nicaragua perform different economic and political roles in the world. As will be shown, these differences have created important constraints and possibilities in the postrevolutionary period. Although both countries' economic opportunities, as price-takers and technology recipients in a capitalist world economy, are severely limited by patterns of international trade and finance, there is no doubt that Nicaragua, as a small agroexporting country, has had more restricted options. In addition, Nicaragua, located in an area often defined as the "backyard" of the United States, has had less room to maneuver within the bipolar international system. There is, of course, no doubt that Iran has also faced adverse international conditions, represented in falling oil prices and the war with Iraq. But its more secure base for capital accumulation, its sheer size, and its geopolitical importance to both superpowers have given it more options. The revolutionary leadership's inability to use these opportunities to enhance Iran's economic prospects, I argue, is a reflection of the way the postrevolutionary state was constituted. Favorable international circumstances were nevertheless important in helping the regime's political survival, despite its inability to restructure economic relationships.

Politics of State Control

How did the Islamic activists and the Sandinista leadership manage to consolidate their control of the state in their respective countries? As mentioned, the answer to this question sets the ideological and political boundaries within which revolutionary outcomes in Iran and Nicaragua can be understood. The major contention of this chapter is that the struggle to gain control of the state took different forms in these two countries, and this difference, in turn, can partially explain the disparate results.

In Iran, two basic processes arising out of the collapse of the Pahlavi dynasty intersected to shape the immediate outcome of the revolution: the struggles among various intermediate classes to build hegemony through the control of the state apparatus and the attendant grass-roots pressure for a more radical socioeconomic transformation. As mentioned in the second chapter, the intermediate classes spearheaded the movement that overthrew the shah in the cities. It was therefore only natural for the different intermediate classes, through their organizational expressions, to vie for hegemony. The Provisional Revolutionary Government (PRG) installed in the immediate postrevolutionary period was essentially a reformist government influenced by organizations that had traditionally been connected to the salaried/professional intermediate class.[22] This early edge, however, was counteracted by the inability of the state to control popular revolutionary organizations, which began to germinate with the unleashing of revolutionary fervor. These organizations challenged the authority of the PRG and its prime minister, Mehdi Bazargan, from many directions.

A multitude of political parties and groups advocated radical policies that ranged from giving autonomy to ethnic groups to disbanding the military. Ethnic uprisings were common, and activists from left-wing political groups attempted to take over factories through the spontaneous creation of workers councils.[23] Some of the left-wing groups furthered their power by controlling a large amount of armament, which they came to possess with their capture of the Tehran arms factory and government arsenal during the last stages of the revolution. According to one study, their public positions suggest they actually envisioned themselves as the core of a popular, revolutionary army that would replace the prerevolutionary armed forces. The establishment of such a popular army and a drastic purge of the prerevolutionary armed forces would have permanently tilted the balance of power toward these armed leftist groups.[24] Since the newly established government did not control these leftist groups, sanctioning their attacks on the military would have undercut the government itself. The PRG's refusal to disband any military organization, with the exception of the small units created for the protection of the shah, was intended not only to retain a professional cadre capable of engaging in modern warfare but also to protect itself against leftist threats.

Another threat to the PRG came from the revolutionary committees, guards, and courts that effectively constituted a rival, extralegal government. These organizations, which were mainly made up of the urban lower strata and the lower ranks of the traditional petty bourgeoisie,[25] were established in government departments, factories, bazaars, and universities, and they gradually appropriated the bulk of actual political power. The

PRG attempted to control them, transfer their power to the government, or dissolve them. None of these strategies worked. These popular organizations had developed a momentum of their own, and they were also sanctioned by other social forces striving for hegemony.

In the previous chapter, I discussed the changes which occurred within the Islamic world view that encouraged part of the clergy to focus on the state in a struggle to achieve hegemony. In this changed world view, the clerics committed to building the Islamic Republic also found justification for employing unlimited means to achieve their ultimate political end on earth.[26] The most important means they employed was sanctioning revolutionary organizations to use violence against political opponents. This enabled the clerics to become fully entrenched as "true" leaders of the revolution and enhance their political resources.

The Revolutionary Council—which, ironically, had drawn up the decree of appointment for the PRG—maintained supreme authority over all popular organizations.[27] In the actual operation of the revolutionary committees, the lower clergy were the most prominent. The same held true for the revolutionary courts, which had usurped the responsibility of executing the old regime's associates.

In short, while the PRG was attempting to demobilize the lower ranks of the politicized population to normalize the situation and keep itself in power, the clergy not only kept them activated but also used cultural and organizational resources to keep these popular sectors under control. In this sense, two bureaucracies—one mass-excluding and one mass-incorporating—were operating at the same time. Clerical control over the mass-incorporating bureaucracy was furthered by the creation of the Islamic Republican Party (IRP). The IRP, founded by the clerics of the Revolutionary Council, was supposed to be a highly structured and disciplined party giving ideological direction to the extralegal bureaucracy. More fundamental, the founding of the IRP openly signaled the leading clerics' desire and capacity to compete directly with the PRG for power. The result was a *controlled* attack against the PRG and the salaried/professional intermediate class associated with it. Because it was unable to prevent arrests, confiscations, execution, suppression of the press, or disruption of political meetings, the PRG could not escape having its flimsy political base swept away as social conflict deepened and disorder spread. It is true that Bazargan stepped down only after the takeover of the U.S. embassy and the revelation, through translated embassy documents, that contacts had been made between U.S. officials and members of his government. It is also true, however, that his efforts to introduce normalcy into a revolutionary situation had already proven futile.

Bazargan's resignation clearly shattered the reformist forces' hope of dominating the state. With their defeat, the IRP could now turn its attention toward the other contenders for power. The leftist political parties and organizations had functioned as an unexpected political ally of the IRP by continuously challenging the PRG, but their political presence was no longer needed or accepted. One of these organizations, the Islamic-leaning Mojahedin-e Khalq, was particularly singled out since it contended directly for power. The organization's oppositional activities were essentially premised on its correct perception that its survival would be threatened by the IRP's dominating state power. Numerically, the Mojahedin was larger than other leftist organizations and more threatening to the IRP because of its similar social base.[28] Nevertheless, its challenge ultimately proved futile.

Despite the fact that the IRP was not in full control of the government, it had already become the most important power broker in Iranian politics. It controlled the prime ministership and Parliament and, hence, was able continuously to challenge the authority of the first president of the Islamic Republic, Abol-Hassan Bani Sadr, who was getting close to the Mojahedin to broaden his support. In addition, the IRP's infiltration of the U.S. embassy, and the utter failure of governmental forces connected to Bani Sadr to do likewise, simply amplified the government's weakness. The Iraqi invasion of Iran also increased the IRP's power, as the closely connected Revolutionary Guard expanded its ranks, improved training, and strengthened its command structure. The war, according to Shaul Bakhash, allowed the revolutionary committees to constitute themselves as the guardians of the revolution against subversives and use this new role as a way to attack internal opposition.[29] Using all these resources, the IRP was easily able to bring about the dismissal of Bani Sadr and crush in a bloody manner the Mojahedin's "armed uprising" in support of his presidency. Bani Sadr's dismissal and the Mojahedin's defeat marked the end of a era characterized by competition for state power and the beginning of an era dominated by the IRP.

Unlike in Iran, competition for state power in Nicaragua was already over by the time Somoza fled the country. To be sure, as mentioned in chapter 2, the bourgeoisie and its organizational expressions, UDEL and FAO, had been important in creating the revolutionary conjuncture. However, the inability, even with U.S. support, to extract the smallest concessions from Somoza caused the bourgeois opposition to lose all possibility of preventing Sandinista leadership of the struggle. In addition, the willingness of the FSLN guerrillas to engage in fixed-location warfare against the National Guard was crucial in securing the FSLN's leadership in the insurrectionary period that lay ahead. By the end of 1978, most of the leadership of the leading political and labor organizations had thrown their support behind the FSLN, which by then had succeeded in unifying its three tendencies or factions under a nine-member supreme command (the FSLN National Directorate—DNC). Hence, as Stephen Gorman aptly points out, "for all practical purposes, the bourgeoisie was forced to accept the Sandinista demand that the dictatorship and its National Guard be completely destroyed, and not merely restructured under the U.S. mediation."[30]

The Sandinista victory over the structure of political and military institutions was an important one.[31] By replacing the National Guard with the Popular Sandinista Army, organized around a core of FSLN guerrilla veterans and Sandinista-led popular militia, the bourgeoisie was effectively cut off from the military.[32] The same was done with the police force. Police and State Security Forces, which had been a part of the National Guard under Somoza, were institutionally separated from the army and put under the Ministry of Interior. In addition, grass-roots groups were organized to defend the revolution. Politically, by promoting the creation of new popular entities—like the Sandinista Defense Committees and the Association of Rural Workers—and endeavoring to increase their representation in the new government, the FSLN effectively prevented the bourgeois opposition from using their government positions to preempt leftist leadership of the popular organizations.

In short, once Somoza was deposed, the DNC was able to establish its control over the composition of the new government while avoiding the use of openly authoritarian tactics. At this point, the struggle was over the ideological direction of the new government. The presence of moderate and conservative forces in the new government and the perceived existence of a social-democratic tendency within the FSLN itself led some observers to worry about the leftist elements' gradually losing power over the policy process.[33] But this did not happen because a political unity against the bourgeois forces was necessary to complete the FSLN's consolidation of power. The supposedly social-democratic faction of the Sandinista Front understood that a move to the right, allowing the bourgeoisie to rebuild its power base, would have prevented all Sandinista factions from sharing power in the long run. On the other hand, a move to the left, with all its attendant political and administrative restructuring, maintained the prerevolutionary unity of the FSLN and ensured that the political clout of the bourgeoisie would be kept under control. The bourgeoisie could become a partner in running the country but only under the hegemony of the FSLN. Those who could not accept the FSLN's control over the policy process left the country and with the help of the United States staged a vicious counterrevolutionary war.[34] Others who remained inside, however, had to negotiate on Sandinista terms. The Sandinistas, in turn, did not have to deal with the bourgeois opposition in overtly harsh terms because of their politically and militarily superior position from the beginning.

Constraints and Possibilities

So far, in explaining the direction of postrevolutionary politics in Iran and Nicaragua, I have focused on the internal struggle to control and maintain state power. To be sure, the way power was consolidated created the ideological and political boundaries within which the new Iranian and Nicaraguan leaders were going to operate. But, with their consolidation of power, the game was not over. These new leaders also had to face constraints and possibilities arising from the preexisting political, economic, and cultural structures as situated within the world context. The boundaries established by the postrevolutionary power struggle thus had to be constantly renegotiated, leaving room for expansion as well as contraction.

The Iranian leadership faced better options in the global economy than did its counterpart in Nicaragua. In fact, like the state the Islamic revolutionaries inherited from the previous regime, the Iranian economy proved very useful in efficiently crushing opponents and maintaining power. In comparison to other countries that have gone through social revolutions, postrevolutionary Iran benefited from a relatively resilient economy. There is no doubt that the economy was beset with significant problems, such as inflationary pressures, intersectoral imbalances, and administrative inefficiencies. Nevertheless, Iran's foreign-exchange reserves stood at $12 to 14 billion, and these were backed by considerable foreign investments, gold holdings, and other assets.[35] These resources allowed the Islamic revolutionaries to gather support among the lower ranks of the population by instituting social programs, such as widespread distribution of food and some reallocation of housing through their social networks.[36] The existence of a relatively robust economy took away the immediate need to change the structure of the Iranian economy to satisfy the needs of those who had become mobilized during the revolution. With the added cost of the Iran-Iraq war, of course, it became increasingly difficult, if not impossible, to satisfy the mobilized population. Furthermore, economic conditions in general began to deteriorate. Yet there has not been much change in policies related to the economy.

Much of the answer to why this is so can be found in the pattern of revolutionary mobilization and the internal stalemate that developed due to the class relations of the revolution. In this regard, two characteristics are particularly important and need to be reiterated. First, there was an almost total absence of rural mobilization. The Iranian Revolution not only was urban in the early stages but also failed to spread substantially to the rural areas in the later stages. In the few areas where noticeable peasant activity in the form of land seizures did take place, it was done either spontaneously or with the help of leftist groups. Mobilization thus occurred in an oppositional context, and, accordingly, the government moved swiftly and successfully to crush these isolated peasant uprisings, which had no national organizational backbone. Given the low level of rural mobilization, this was not a major endeavor. However, the absence of a coherent rural project, occasioned by the lack of a rural constituency, left a lasting imprint on the Iranian Revolution.

The second reason for a stalemate in economic decision making relates to the sources of support for the revolutionaries. As mentioned earlier, in their political coalition to topple the shah, the Islamic revolutionaries drew most of their power and financial resources from the merchant and bazaar classes. In supporting the revolution, the merchants were acting out of mixed motives. They resented their loss of status, competition from foreign industries, and excessive concentration of economic power in the hands of a privileged few. They were also weary of excessive government regulation of commerce and belated attempts to increase taxes. They envisioned good government as one that protected private property, freed them from government restrictions and controls, provided them with greater business opportunities, and taxed them lightly. The clerics, however, found it difficult to follow this vision fully since their success was also due to their ability to generate support from popular organizations. Also, to maintain their hegemony over the subordinate classes, they created a number of populist organizations to administer and pursue social welfare and reconstruction programs—e.g., Jahad-e Sazandegi (Crusade for Constructiveness) and Bonyad-e Mostazefin (Foundation for the Downtrodden). Once instituted, these organizations began to generate demands representing their constituencies. In their attempt to maintain the support of popular organizations, as Hossein Bashiriyeh succinctly points out, "the fundamentalist clergy articulated a state ideology imbued with populism. It advocated redistributive policies and sought to antagonize the lower classes against the *mostakbarin* (predators)."[37]

The consequence of this populist strategy was a very peculiar relationship with the bazaar community. Clearly, many members of the community were absorbed into the revolutionary organizations and the government. But because of the objective position they occupied as members of a populist state, they began to act contrary to the interests of the stratum or class from which they came. Their actions were especially detrimental to the interests of large merchants and even the middle traders and artisans.[38] At the same time, however, the regime was not able to rid itself of its bazaari roots. The result was a continuous conflict between interest and ideology *within* the government, with the consequent stalemate over the issue of socioeconomic reforms.

This conflict was accentuated by another related contradiction originating in the postrevolutionary political structure: the dual structure of governance.[39] As mentioned, the Islamic revolutionaries found the preexisting state structure useful in consolidating their power; hence, they saw no need to dismantle the old structure and replace it with a new one. Decapitation was deemed sufficient. While considerable upheaval engulfed bureaucracies during the process of stripping away the upper echelons of the civil service, the apparatus itself remained in place. Interestingly, but perhaps not surprisingly, the bureaucratic maxim of operating on the basis of regulations and procedures was a moderating check on the new men who took over the state apparatus. But because of popular mobilization, the new leaders were also forced to leave their own distinctive imprints. The new popular organizations usurped some of the functions of the existing bureaucracies. The more common outcome, however, was the duplication of functions, with resultant jurisdictional tensions.

The founders of the IRP had hoped to overcome these tensions, and the one between interest and ideology, through the creation of the party. By locating the party above the state in a political bureau, the IRP expected strong identification to develop between the state and the party. As in the Soviet Union, the rationalization for the creation of this link was to control the abuses and to give ideological direction to the state. In the case of the Soviet Union, in practice the party became identified with the state, and the bureaucracy ended up being a filter that stopped communication between the leaders and the people. In the Iranian case, the IRP became the arbiter between the state and the popular organizations. This, in turn, ended up reproducing the tensions mentioned above within the IRP itself. It was perhaps its inability to control conflicts that led Khomeini to suspend the IRP's activities in 1989.[40]

To be sure, conflict did not characterize all decision-making processes. For instance, there was hardly any disagreement on the need for maintaining Islamic norms of social and gender relations, education, ethics, and law. There is no doubt that, precisely because of this unity, the regime was much more effective in instituting major change in these areas.[41] As shown in the previous chapter, this unity was a result of a pattern of ideological mobilization that established the shah as the source of Western values and envisioned the opposition's task as one of reinstating Islamic cultural codes. Clearly, this process did not create space for unity on economic and political grounds.

A different dynamic was at work in Nicaragua. The process of ideological mobilization did not create similar unity on cultural grounds. If anything, the heritage of a Christian-Marxist dialogue continued to generate conflicts and disagreements. At the same time, however, these disagreements, based on comparable strength of both traditions, created space for negotiation. Political tolerance of other points of view was made possible by the existence of a fundamentally religious conception of the world, which was rooted in popular belief but was ideologically independent of the FSLN.

The Nicaraguan revolutionaries also behaved differently in the economic realm as they moved swiftly to leave their imprint. All the properties of Somoza, his family, his close allies, and the high-ranking military were immediately confiscated (approximately 25 percent of industrial plants and 21 percent of the area under cultivation). The expropriated lands were large, modern farms, located on prime agricultural land in the developed Pacific region. They produced export crops and, hence, were an important source of foreign exchange. These farms were organized as farms within the "Area of People's Property (APP)." In addition, the new government nationalized the banking and insurance systems because the latter was unable to cope with the needs of a war-ravished country and because the former had simply played too large a role in the corrupt economic system of the previous regime.[42] Control of banking and foreign trade certainly enabled the state to limit the earnings of families who dominated the export sector. To prevent agroexport production from collapsing, however, the state felt that it had to make sufficient concessions to large producers and exporters of agricultural products. According to Forrest Colburn, this meant generous credit and price concessions to large producers and no wage increases for labor.[43]

Why didn't the revolutionary forces immediately attack large producers as their populist rhetoric would suggest? Is it that they did not have the power to do so? Given the extent of political consolidation by the FSLN, I do not think that this question can be resolved simply in terms of political power. Several conditions under which the new regime came to power can give us better clues. First, the FSLN had a close affinity with the cities. While this did not make the FSLN anti-peasant, it inhibited its understanding of the complexity of the rural class structure. The rural problem was mostly seen from the point of view of promoting adequate production. Many members of the FSLN felt that, given the extent of damages suffered by the Nicaraguan economy during the insurrection, it would be suicidal to undermine the economy's source of foreign exchange. This is why, in addition to compromising with large producers, the FSLN generally did not even break up the modern commercial farms confiscated from the Somocistas and distribute them to peasants, as expected. According to one source, "The state farms were identified as preferable for administrative and investment purposes, as well as a way to allow income to be shared socially. Any surplus produced by the farms would flow directly to the state and serve the nation as a whole."[44] Meanwhile, stagnant peasant producers were going to be rapidly converted to a "semiproletarian" or fully proletarian labor force.

Second, the fact that a significant share of the state property inherited from Somoza was in financial, rather than productive, sectors meant that the state still lacked direct control of key productive sectors. This perceived weakness gave rise to a strategy of indirect control over key productive sectors through the state's monopoly of credit and control of marketing and foreign trade.[45] The third factor militating against the takeover of the agroexport sector was the weakness of the administrative apparatus at central and local levels. The Somoza state was designed to demobilize the population politically while allowing for private economic pursuits of a few. As such, it was not very well suited to the FSLN's gaining direct control over the private sector and meeting other priorities, such as the reconstruction of urban areas and immediate assistance to the impoverished peasant sector. This is why the regime felt that, to maintain its political and administrative viability, it needed to pursue a policy that attempted to promote an alliance of classes across the socioeconomic spectrum. Administratively, it was thought, Nicaragua simply could not afford to lose the support of the professional class that helped run the postrevolutionary state.

The policy of privileging the large agricultural producers (private and state-controlled) did not go uncontested. Several factors coalesced to push the government to redirect its agricultural policy toward redistribution of land to landless peasants and increased support for the peasant capitalists. The first factor was the political strength of small and medium commercial producers, bolstered by their superior economic performance. Initially, the small and medium producers formed, with the help of the FSLN and Christian volunteers, the Association of Rural Workers Association (ATC); however, the affiliation of thousands of producers with a predominantly workers' organization was simply too divisive. In 1981, instead of joining the Union of Nicaraguan Agricultural Producers (UPANIC), which was dominated by large producers, the small and medium producers organized themselves into the National Union of Farmers and Ranchers (UNAG).[46] After that, the Sandinistas increasingly recognized the complexity of

Nicaragua's agrarian structure and the importance of peasant producers' perspectives. The political strength of the small and medium producers was complemented by their economic performance. David Kaimowitz nicely compares their economic performance to the results in state and large farms:

> Economically, the small and medium commercial producers were the suc-
> cess story of the revolution. Their weight in agricultural production grew
> significantly in the first years of the revolution, not only in basic grains but
> in traditional agroexport crops as well. This expansion was particularly
> outstanding in the case of beans and cotton. Investments by peasant
> capitalists and small farmers were also 'cheaper' for the government. Unlike
> the state and large private sector which relied almost exclusively on public
> credit for investment, these producers engaged in a substantial amount of
> self-generated investment. Per *cordoba* of output produced they also used
> less foreign exchange because of their lower reliance on imported agricul-
> tural inputs and machinery. This was in sharp contrast with the experience
> in both the state and large private sector. In 1980 the state incurred large
> losses and while state farm production rose rapidly over the following
> years, costs were higher than in the private sector and many state farms
> were in a state of virtual default with respect to their loans. . . . Nor was
> there much expansion on the large private farms (with some exceptions in
> the case of sugar and rice). Despite economic incentives from the govern-
> ment large private producers continued to be reluctant to invest their own
> money because of perceived threats of future expropriation or instability.[47]

The second important reason for a shift in policy toward peasant producers and landless peasants was the political and economic world context. According to Kaimowitz, even with the political strength of small and medium farmers and their superior economic performance, there still might not have been a change in policy had it not been for the U.S. war against Nicaragua.[48] The war, which began to escalate in 1982, required the full support of the previously neglected peasantry and rural landless in the areas of military conflict. It also brought to fore the need to give more attention to food self-sufficiency. All this slowly introduced into the postrevolutionary discourse the view that peasant cooperatives were a progressive form of production appropriate to Nicaraguan condi-tions.[49] To be sure, it did not become dominant, but the need to reap the military benefits of peasant satisfaction allowed the FSLN, at least temporarily, to overcome some of the worries about these measures slowing agricultural modernization and creating labor shortages for the agroexporting sector.[50]

State-farm holdings (as well as some landholdings in the capitalist livestock sector) were reduced, while producer cooperatives, composed primarily of formerly landless workers who were engaged in petty and communal grain production for internal consumption, increased.[51] In addition, support increased for peasant capitalists and small independent commercial producers, particularly for those living in areas of military conflict. This does not mean that the FSLN abandoned large producers. The central role of the agroexport sector in the overall functioning of the economy and the traditionally negative attitudes regarding the economic capabilities of the peasantry continued to generate a desire to protect the functioning of that sector at all cost. But, petty production was added to communal production as an acceptable alternative to state farms. The side by side existence of large and petty-commodity production along with communal and state farms clearly opens interesting questions about the political future of Nicaragua. Whether or not this tenuous balance can be sustained much longer, there is no doubt that this complex and somewhat unique result can only be explained by understanding the class relations of the revolution and the international context that has impinged on the agroexporting economy of Nicaragua.

Summing Up

The changes wrought by the Iranian and Nicaraguan revolutions have not run their course, but I have attempted to demonstrate that the kind of changes that have taken place so far and their differences can be explained through an analysis of forces that shaped the causes and processes of these revolutions. More specifically, revolutionary outcomes in Iran and Nicaragua were powerfully shaped by the political struggle to control and maintain state power. In Iran, the state structure was largely kept in tact to control threats from the left, while in Nicaragua a complete overhaul was necessary to tame the bourgeois forces. At the same time, however, the boundaries created by this struggle over state power were, and continue to be, renegotiated due to the process of ideological mobilization, the class relations of the revolution, and the international context. In Nicaragua, this meant a more tolerant political environment and economic and social policies that were more pro-peasant and decentralized, in the midst of a severe economic crisis largely caused by a hostile international environment. In Iran, on the other hand, conflicts generated by a contradictory social base essentially prevented the articulation of a coherent economic policy initially, while the war with Iraq drained enough resources to propel Iran into a serious economic crisis. The Iranian revolutionaries have been able to implement their Islamic project in the cultural arena only because of the unity created through the process of ideological mobilization.

The Iranian and Nicaraguan revolutions have produced important discontinuities, yet they also reflect continuities. The inability to break out of the mold of export-oriented economies is an important continuity for both countries, while cultural innovations in Iran and economic and political restructuring in Nicaragua represent important discontinuities. The extent to which these discontinuities can be deepened will continue to depend on the revolutionary class configuration, the international environment, and the interaction among them.

NOTES

1. The irony cannot be missed, particularly in the case of Iran where the so-called fundamentalist forces were able to create a more "modern" state, with highly differentiated political structures, than the one built by the so-called modernist monarch. Hence, we see in Iran today a fairly developed parliamentary system, which continues to deny its citizens basic political rights but is, nevertheless, composed of strong, independent, and competing political institutions. In other words, the new dictatorship, which in many ways has been more repressive and violent than the previous one, also gave birth to political institutions that do not operate solely on the basis of decisions made by one person.

2. The most drastic change came about in the judiciary, where a harsh system of justice based on Islamic principles and administered by Islamic judges has been instituted. The Revolutionary Courts, which were independent entities, originally administered the justice system, but they were absorbed into the Ministry of Justice by 1984.

3. A. Bayat, "Workers' Control after the Revolution," MERIP [Middle East Research and Information Project] Reports 13, 3 (1983), pp. 19–23.

4. J. Paul, "Iran's Peasants and the Revolution: An Introduction," MERIP Reports 12, 3 (1982), pp. 22–23.

5. For an excellent study of political consolidation in the postrevolutionary period, see S. Bakhash, The Reign of the Ayatollahs (New York: Basic Books, 1984).

6. Revolutionary Guards were transformed into the Ministry of Revolutionary Guards, signaling the permanence of this force in the regime's security apparatus.

7. In 1986, the figures released by the regime on income distribution showed that the top 20 percent of population was receiving 50 percent of the national income. This indicates very little headway in the effort to equalize class differences. See S. Akhavi, "Institutionalizing the New Order in Iran," Current History 86 (February 1987), p. 55.

8. F. Fesharaki, "Observations on Iran, Saudi Arabia, and the Oil Market," unpublished paper, East-West Center, University of Hawaii at Manoa, Honolulu, November, 1986. Fesharaki also reports that, given the damages incurred by Iraqi hits on Iranian refineries, Iran was forced to import 160,000 barrels a day

(mainly diesel and kerosene) for domestic consumption. Furthermore, the Iranian crude oil exports for 1986 fell to 1.09 million barrels a day (mbd), down from 1.35 mbd in 1985. In addition, given the dramatic drop in oil prices, the total value of oil revenues dropped from $12.5 billion in 1985 to an estimated $4.8 billion in 1986.

9. S. M. Gorman, "Power and Consolidation in the Nicaraguan Revolution," *Journal of Latin American Studies* 13, 1 (1981), pp. 133–49.

10. For an enlightening analysis of the competition between the "popular" and Catholic churches, see C. C. O'Brien, "God and Man in Nicaragua," *The Atlantic Monthly* 258 (August 1986), pp. 50–72.

11. See the discussion of Nicaragua's economy in R. L. Harris, "The Revolutionary Transformation of Nicaragua," *Latin American Perspectives* 14, 1 (1987), pp. 8–10.

12. R. L. Harris, "The Revolutionary Process in Nicaragua," *Latin American Perspectives* 12, 2 (1985), p. 10.

13. G. Irwin, "Nicaragua: Establishing the State as the Centre of Accumulation," *Cambridge Journal of Economics* 7, 2 (1983), p. 127.

14. Agriculture generates 70.6 percent of Nicaragua's foreign-exchange earnings. Quoted in L. J. Enriquez, "Half a Decade of Sandinista Policy-Making: Recent Publications on Revolutionary Policies in Contemporary Nicaragua," *Latin American Research Review* 22, 3 (1987), p. 221, n. 5.

15. Somoza holdings taken over by the state represented about 20 percent of all agricultural land but accounted for some 47 percent of all land in farms larger than 350 hectares, including most of the country's most capital-intensive and modern farms. See D. Kaimowitz, "Nicaraguan Debates on Agrarian Structure and Their Implications for Agricultural Policy and the Rural Poor," *Journal of Peasant Studies* 14 (October 1986), pp. 106–7.

16. Between 1982 and 1984, land in production cooperatives rose from 2 percent to 10 percent. For detailed analysis of these policy changes, see ibid., pp. 111–13.

17. C. D. Deere, P. Marchetti, and N. Reinhardt, "The Peasantry and the Development of Sandinista Agrarian Policy, 1979–1984," *Latin America Research Review*, 20, 3 (1985), p. 103. For similar assessments on the influential role played by organizations representing peasants and rural workers, see ibid., and I. Luciak, "National Unity and Popular Hegemony: The Dialectics of Sandinista Agrarian Reform Policies, 1979–1986," *Journal of Latin American Studies* 19 (May 1987), pp. 113–40.

18. T. Skocpol, *States and Social Revolutions: A Comparative Analysis of France, Russia and China* (Cambridge: Cambridge University Press, 1979), pp. 164–65.

19. The literature on revolutionary outcomes has been sufficiently aware of the role of existing economic and political structures and the international context in preventing the revolutionaries from pursuing their "idealistic" projects. After all, it is not very outlandish to claim that revolutionaries do not inherit a clean slate. Much more debatable is the role of ideological structures and the class

relations of the revolution itself. This is why the theoretical argument that follows focuses mostly on these two aspects. Of course, in the discussion of Iran and Nicaragua, I elaborate on all of the constraints mentioned.

20. Nicaragua's willingness to negotiate over the question of internal democracy within the context of the Esquipulas II Plan reflected the relative openness of Sandinistas. I cannot think of another postrevolutionary regime that has been willing to do the same.

21. On the role of mass military mobilization in helping the consolidation of authoritarian revolutionary regimes, see T. Skocpol, "Social Revolutions and Mass Military Mobilization," *World Politics* 40, 2 (1988), pp. 147–68.

22. The PRG was appointed by Khomeini. The decree of appointment was drawn up by the Revolutionary Council and signed by Khomeini. On the makeup of the Revolutionary Council, see note 27.

23. S. Azad, "Workers' and Peasants' Councils in Iran," *Monthly Review* 32, 5 (1980), pp. 14–29.

24. G. F. Rose, "The Post-Revolutionary Purge of Iran's Armed Forces: A Revisionist Assessment," *Iranian Studies* 17, 2–3 (1984), pp. 155–56.

25. H. Bashiriyeh, *State and Revolution in Iran, 1962–1982* (New York: St. Martin's Press, 1984), pp. 134–35.

26. It is important to emphasize that not all the clerics should be categorized as supporters of the Islamic Republic. Many supported the PRG and with its demise lost their political power.

27. The Revolutionary Council was established by Khomeini as the monarchy fell. It originally included representatives of both salaried and traditional intermediate classes. With the formation of the PRG, however, Bazargan and six of his colleagues left to form the cabinet. The overall effect was to strengthen the clerics vying for the establishment of an Islamic republic. See Bakhash, *The Reign of the Ayatollahs*, chapter 3.

28. The Islamic orientation of the Mojahedin can help explain its appeal. Other leftist organizations (mostly Marxist-Leninist) posed less of a threat due to their small size. They were all crushed in time. The Moscow-oriented Tudeh party's position was different since it wholeheartedly supported IRP policies. It was nevertheless purged in 1983, after its members were accused of being spies for the Soviet Union.

29. Bakhash, *The Reign of the Ayatollahs*, p. 128. Since Bani Sadr was the chair of the Supreme Defense Council, his power was also enhanced by the war. But, essentially, his presidency was made possible because of Ayatollah Khomeini's support. Once Khomeini withdrew his support because of Bani Sadr's flirtation with the Mojahedin, the way was cleared for Bani Sadr's dismissal.

30. Gorman, "Power and Consolidation in the Nicaraguan Revolution," p. 136.

31. The FSLN's victory over the structure of political and military institutions was very much aided by Somoza's decision to make the revolutionary confrontation a bloody one. As mentioned in chapter 2, the National Guard's violence made its suspension unavoidable.

32. The following information about the structure of political and military institutions is taken from Gorman, "Power and Consolidation in the Nicaraguan Revolution."

33. See J. Petras, "Whither the Nicaraguan Revolution?" *Monthly Review* 31, 5 (1979), pp. 1–22.

34. Clearly, the counterrevolutionary forces have been very successful in terms of creating economic chaos and causing irreparable physical damage. They have also been effective at causing perhaps irreversible damage to the revolutionary spirit of the Nicaraguans.

35. M. Khadim, *The Political Economy of Revolutionary Iran* (Cairo: Cairo Papers in Social Science, 1983), p. 47.

36. It is important to note that the distribution of social goods was generally undertaken by popular organizations, such as the local revolutionary committees. These were, of course, the same organizations involved in mobilization and political control. This meant that the loyalty of recipients could be used as a condition for favors. On this, see A. Vali and S. Zubaida, "Factionalism and Political Discourse in Islamic Republic of Iran: The Case of Hujjatiyeh Society," *Economy and Society* 14, 2 (1985), pp. 139–73.

37. Bashiriyeh, *State and Revolution in Iran*, p. 171.

38. See the interview with A. Ashraf in *MERIP Reports*, no. 113 (March–April 1983), pp. 16–18.

39. My discussion of the dual structure of governance borrows from an illuminating discussion in Bakhash, *The Reign of the Ayatollahs*, chapter 10.

40. In their request to suspend the IRP, President Mohammad Ali Khamenei and Majles Speaker Ali Akhbar Hashemi-Rafsanjani, surviving founders of the IRP, suggested that the party had achieved its purpose of establishing the distinctive institutions of the Islamic Republic and its activities would henceforth have a divisive effect on the community. See S. A. Arjomand, *The Turban for the Crown* (New York: Oxford University Press, 1988), p. 169. Recently, political parties have been allowed to register and vie for public support, but none of them has yet emerged as a dominant force.

41. According to Akhavi, "This unity of the clergy over cultural issues leads many observers to call the Iranian events above all a cultural revolution. It also explains why outside observers sometimes ascribe to the leadership a monolithic pattern of thought and conduct in the political and economic spheres. But unity in cultural matters does not automatically translate into unity on political and economic issues." Akhavi, "Institutionalizing the New Order in Iran," p. 55.

42. F. Colburn, *Post-Revolutionary Nicaragua: State, Class, and the Dilemmas of Agrarian Policy* (Berkeley: University of California Press, 1986), p. 123.

43. Ibid, p. 124.

44. M. Zalkin, "Food Policy and Class Transformation in Revolutionary Nicaragua, 1979–86," *World Development* 15, 7 (1987), p. 93. It is important to point out that initially the FSLN had good reason to think policies emphasizing state farms and large farmers would not harm others. With the rapid recovery

from the destruction and dislocations created by the 1979 war and the large quantities of foreign aid flowing into the country, economic decision making was not a zero-sum game. See Kaimovitz, "Nicaraguan Debates on Agrarian Structure," pp. 105–7.

45. Irwin, "Nicaragua," p. 128.

46. For an enlightening analysis of UNAG's struggle to assert itself, see I. A. Luciak, "Popular Democracy in the New Nicaragua: The Case of a Rural Mass Organization," *Comparative Politics* 20, 1 (1987), pp. 35–55.

47. Kaimowitz, "Nicaraguan Debates on Agrarian Structure," p. 111.

48. Ibid., pp. 111–13. Between 1982 and 1988, the war caused an estimated $3.5 billion in economic destruction. The contras made targets of agricultural cooperatives and state farms, causing a serious drop in food production. All this caused the government to spend a full 50 percent of its budget on the war effort. Reported in M. Massing, "Who Are the Sandinistas?" *New York Review of Books* (May 12, 1988), p. 56. The economic crisis generated by this military aggression was accentuated by falling international prices for Nicaragua's agroexports, Washington's efforts to prevent the revolutionary government from obtaining loans and credits from international lending sources, and the U.S. trade embargo.

49. In this sense, Reagan's aggressive policy to "stop communism" ironically further radicalized the revolution.

50. Persistent worries about labor shortages for the cotton and coffee harvests and lack of confidence in the peasant's traditional technology and culture were, of course, part of the anti-peasant legacy of agroexport agriculture established well before the revolution.

51. See N. Reinhardt, "Agro-Exports and the Peasantry in the Agrarian Reforms of El Salvador and Nicaragua," *World Development* 15, 7 (1987), pp. 941–59.

Conclusion

I began this project with the intention of trying to understand how the growth and form of the national state and the development of capitalism on the world scale interacted to alter the ways in which ordinary people banded together to act on their perceived interests. Understanding the specific interaction of class and state structures as situated within the global states and economic systems has been the guiding principle throughout this endeavor. The Iranian and Nicaraguan cases were used to shed light on revolutionary processes in societies with relatively high degrees of urbanization. These two cases were also utilized to gain an understanding of the type of state that is particularly susceptible to sociorevolutionary upheavals in these societies. The following is a synopsis of my findings about Iran and Nicaragua:[1]

1. The sociostructural and world-historical underpinnings of the Iranian and Nicaraguan economic systems made the coalescence of diverse urban oppositional groupings *possible* by:

  a. developing an economically interventionist state which, as the manager of the means of daily life, had become not only the distributor of favors to the population but also the source of grievances;

  b. giving preference to a kind of development that made incorporation into the international division of labor as exporters of primary products more important than the development of more diversified national capital;

  c. giving the intermediate classes a strategic field in the economy and polity and thus endowing them with the potential to play a hegemonic role in the construction of political reaction to the shah's and Somoza's regimes; and

d. causing a rapid and disorienting process of urbanization which created a population that could be mobilized.

2. Since most of these factors are present in many other peripheral formations, they cannot be considered the structural factors that allowed the coalescence of urban groupings to become *actualized*. In this study, I demonstrated that the actualization of opposition was related to:

a. the disjunction between the ruling cliques and the intermediate classes. In both countries, the method of governance prohibited autonomous political organization and antagonized the professional/salaried class—precisely the class that had begun to gain economic and political capabilities through the promoted pattern of industrialization. In Nicaragua, the opponents even included the bourgeoisie. The distinguishing feature of Iran was, of course, the important presence of the traditional petty bourgeoisie that was antagonized both by the shah's industrial policies and by his mode of governance.

b. the clerics' effective use of already existing cultural networks in Iran, and the FSLN's linkages with the religiously based organizations in Nicaragua. In addition to the organizational networks offered to the revolutionaries, Islam and the Christian-Marxist dialogue were helpful in offering a medium through which Iranian and Nicaraguan nationalism could be expressed.

3. The actual breakdown of the states and their inability to respond to popular mobilization can be explained by:

a. the structure of the state. The shah's rule, based on economic appeasement of the population, total personal domination, and U.S. support, proved ineffective at the time of economic crisis, personal problems, and domestic bickering over foreign policy in the United States. In Nicaragua, Somoza's attempt to fight his opponents, despite the desertion of the prominent classes and wavering U.S. support, was unsuccessful because of the National Guard's inability to sustain a national counterrevolutionary strategy.

b. the world context, which entailed superpower rivalry, confusion within the U.S. foreign policy establishment, and the U.S. desire to regain ideological hegemony in the world.

4. The postrevolutionary struggle in Iran can be explained in terms of the coincidence of two processes:

a. the struggle among the intermediate classes to gain control of the state; and

    b. the popular mobilization expressed through the creation of revolutionary organizations.

The postrevolutionary struggle in Nicaragua, on the other hand, initially was much less intense since the FSLN had gained hegemony during the struggle to overthrow Somoza.

    5. The immediate postrevolutionary success of revolutionaries in both countries can be attributed to the links to, and the ultimate control of, the revolutionary organizations.

    6. Finally, the continued contradictions plaguing the postrevolutionary regimes can be explained by:

        a. the Iranian regime's inability to reconcile the demands of a populist base with interests requiring the maintenance of order and the protection of private property and the Nicaraguan regime's difficulties in satisfying the interests arising from an agroexporting economy within a hostile international environment;

        b. the additional inability of the Iranian regime, unlike the Nicaraguan regime at least so far, to transcend the dual structure of governance brought forth by the immediate postrevolutionary situation.

This synopsis gives a brief overview of how the Iranian and Nicaraguan revolutions and their aftermaths were approached in this study. The only remaining question is whether this approach adds any valuable insights to the understanding of other revolutionary situations. This is an important question since this study was not intended to offer new evidence about either of these revolutions but to situate the evidence presented by others within the framework for analysis developed in chapter 1. If the argument presented is a solid one, then the reader should find the theoretical framework presented useful for understanding other comparable cases.

In a comparative perspective, the state-centered crises that launched the Iranian and Nicaraguan revolutions bore many similarities to the ones that instigated the Mexican Revolution (1910–20), the Cuban Revolution (1956–59), and the more recent upheaval in the Philippines. These events differed from other revolutions in peripheral formations in that the primary target was not foreign domination but the political and social system of an indigenous ruling class and its allies. These revolutions were located in a new time, one that began with the postcolonial era. Of course, the societies in which these revolutions originated differed in the level of socioeconomic growth, the strength of polar classes, and the intensity of social conflict. The states overseeing these societies, however, exhibited common characteristics important in launching each of the revolutionary crises.

First, in all of these societies, personal political machines were enhanced at the expense of liberal institutions, the militaries had become personal appendages, and the techniques of discrediting potential rivals had been carried to the point that the individual leaders had become indispensable for the smooth functioning of the state. Second, all these regimes were characterized by compromises with foreign capital and governments. Two of the dictatorships (Batista's and Marcos's) were directly supported by U.S. policies in their rise to, and consolidation of, power. This source of external assistance in a bipolar international environment helped to detach the repressive states from their social bases and to dispense with the structural reforms other more internationally autonomous regimes would have been forced to make. Mexico's regime was not directly indebted to U.S. presence but was nevertheless constrained by the country's dependence on massive U.S. investment. In each case, the relationship with the United States proved destabilizing in the long run. There was never a systematic U.S. policy to weaken any of these regimes, but the effect of most U.S. actions was the same. In each case, the United States was interested in safeguarding the system of profitable relations. Once a multiclass coalition against the individual leader developed, the United States did not consistently support the individual leaders involved. The hitch in Cuba and Mexico was that the individual leaders had by then become the state. The only exception to this pattern, so far, has been the Philippines, where the United States actively intervened to ensure Marcos's exit, without the disintegration of the state. This favorable outcome, however, was not the result of calculated U.S. planning. Rather, it was made possible by the structure of the Philippine state, which was, and continues to be, much more decentralized and dependent on local networks of political power.[2] The downfall of Marcos in Manila thus did not automatically create a hiatus in the authority structure. To be sure, the 1986 election opened the door for a new leadership, but the presence of the old local networks prevented further radicalization.

Nevertheless, as in Cuba and Mexico, the primary cause of the political crisis that engulfed the state in the Philippines can be found in its inability to juggle interests emanating from an increasingly complicated class structure. It is important that, in all three countries, significant sectors of the local bourgeoisie rallied in the end to support the movements against the dictatorships. The intermediate classes were even more important since the leadership and a significant portion of rank and file were drawn from them. Of course, the context of each state breakdown took a different form. In Mexico, Díaz, faced with a succession crisis, found himself unable to harmonize the interests of the increasingly differentiated bourgeoisie and the ethnically distinct middle strata.[3] In Cuba and the Philippines, the disjunctions between the ruling cliques and the prominent classes were perhaps the most acute. The disjunctions occurred, as in Nicaragua, when the individual leaders and small cliques of corrupt collaborators monopolized economic activity and constrained the opportunity for capital accumulation previously available to other sectors of the bourgeoisie and the propertied intermediate class.[4]

At this point, it is important to note I am not contending that the state is the sole causal agency bringing about revolution. As I demonstrated in chapters 3 and 4, the societal context and the patterns of political and ideological mobilization are necessary ingredients for understanding revolutionary processes and outcomes. But an indispensable part of my argument has been the singling out of a particular type of state as distinctively susceptible to revolution. The adequacy of this argument can be more certain if it can be shown that the highlighted causes also differentiate Iran's and Nicaragua's patterns of social development and crises from patterns in comparable countries that did not experience social revolutionary transformations. I will not engage in a full-fledged attempt to use the "method of difference." The following cases are simply cited as potential future tests of part of my argument.

One example of revolutionary failure was already referred to in the analysis of the Iranian case. Iran experienced another period of extensive popular mobilization during the early 1950s; however, the state did not disintegrate, despite the shah's forced departure. Ironically, it was the challenger to his personal dominance, Mossadeq, who prevented this disintegration, but he did it at the cost of halting popular mobilization and paving the way for the shah's return. The nationalist interlude of the 1950s did contain many similarities to the more recent revolutionary situation. Clearly, the opposition had created a wide base of support among the lower ranks of the society and the intermediate classes. The National Front also represented the national bourgeoisie, which at that time was still struggling to survive. The opposition had also gained international recognition since it actually controlled the state. In a sense, one could argue, Mossadeq, like Bakhtiar, had inherited the state apparatus from the shah and was intent on developing a constitutional regime. Both prime ministers were overthrown. But the overthrow of one led to the reestablishment of a reactionary regime, while the overthrow of the other opened the path for a social revolution.

Despite similarities, there were certain differences that may explain the defeat of the nationalist coalition in the 1950s. The most important

difference lay in the lesser structural role the shah played in the 1950s—
he did not dominate the state as he later did, and, furthermore, the state
did not dominate civil society the way it did subsequently. To rule, the
shah had to develop alliances within the Iranian society. To be sure, the
support for his regime was still limited to a distinct minority in popular
and class terms, but he was able to attain the allegiance and acquiescence
of key elites. For instance, after scrimmages with the landed class, he
managed to gain its support. More important, while his government was
isolated enough to arouse the reformist and revolutionary opposition, it
had not yet developed into the narrow, personalistic clique against which
virtually all in the nation could rally, whatever their economic role and
class position. The fact that there were opposition leaders who could
operate within the governmental framework and challenge the shah
attested to this. The lack of a clear enemy eventually meant that the
opposition movement was unable to maintain its unity against the shah.
The propertied intermediate class thus began to withdraw its support for
Mossadeq, which allowed for the rejuvenation of internal support for
the shah.

The second important difference lay in the international context.
Superpower rivalry and domestic politics in the United States kept the
U.S. government *actively* supportive of the shah, without compromising
the regime's nationalist integrity. It is important to remember that the
United States had managed to portray a neutral stance in the Irano-
British oil dispute. Even Mossadeq had hoped the United States would
use its influence to convince the British to negotiate with Iran. It was this
deep-seated belief that prevented Mossadeq from rapprochement with
the influential communist movement and the Soviet Union. Once the
United States refused to support Mossadeq, he had no leg to stand on.
Without the support of the intermediate classes, the working-class
movement, spearheaded by the communist Tudeh party, was also crushed
by the Iranian military and its U.S. backers.

Another interesting contrast is the revolutionary situation in El
Salvador. El Salvador is a country that has experienced one of the highest
levels of revolutionary mobilization in Latin America. The Salvadoran
revolutionaries appear to have substantial peasant support and a comparatively large armed forces. Yet winning state power has proved to be
very difficult. As in the successful revolutionary cases, the Salvadoran
situation can be explained by the relationship of the state to the class
structure.

The Salvadoran state has been dominated by the military since
1931, when the hegemony of the coffee oligarchy was threatened by
economic crisis and lower-class mobilization.[5] Until recently, a succes-

sion of military regimes has ruled, rigidly protecting the extant class structure and suppressing attempts for socioeconomic and political reform. José Napoleón Duarte's regime tried to introduce minor economic and political reforms in response to revolutionary upheavals, thus evoking the hostility of many members of the upper class. In general, the Salvadoran state has been an instrument of class domination. The Duarte government's attempt to exercise autonomy from the dominant class was made possible only by the U.S. insistence on creating a "viable center."[6]

Because of its blatant forms of inequality and domination, the state in El Salvador has been faced with redistribution pressures from below. But, unlike in Nicaragua, the state has maintained upper-class support. The strength of the upper class in El Salvador vis-à-vis the state has offered the former the possibility of dominating the state. This has given the upper class little incentive for desertions to the revolutionary movement. If anything, revolutionary pressures from below have solidified upper-class support for the state. Meanwhile, given the high degree of polarization, the intermediate classes have been fractionalized and driven to the pole of either reaction or revolution. Unlike the intermediate classes in Iran and Nicaragua, they have sought direction from the polar classes. Finally, in the aftermath of the Iranian and Nicaraguan revolutions and a change of administration in the United States, a key foreign government has actively opposed the revolutionary movement. This has given the state another bulwark of support to prevent its disintegration.

Taken together, these factors suggest important elements for revolutionary success are missing. Although active mobilization continues, these factors have prevented the breakdown of the state. The result has been a war of attrition and protracted struggle. Unlike mobilization efforts in Iran and Nicaragua, urban mass demonstrations and general strikes in El Salvador have failed over the last few years, mostly as a result of the government's strong repressive measures. This, however, does not necessarily mean the revolution cannot succeed in El Salvador. In fact, in the past few years, the relationship between the state and the upper class has become much more tenuous as U.S. pressures forced Duarte's regime to introduce a modicum of social and political change. The recent installation of a right-wing government might have eased that tension a bit. Nevertheless, at this point, there appears to be little doubt that only U.S. military and financial assistance will prevent the disintegration of the state in the face of active mobilization on the part of the FMLN (Farabundo Martí National Liberation Front). Any wavering in that support will undoubtedly bring about its long-expected breakdown.

A Reassessment of Skocpol's Approach

I began this study with the assertion that Skocpol's methodological approach must be taken seriously. I agreed with her that the causes and outcome of any revolution must be understood by looking at the specific interaction of class and state structures and the complex interplay of domestic and international developments. The preceding chapters have reflected my indebtedness to this general principle. However, this indebtedness is to a "general" principle, since I have also found it difficult to apply her specific explanatory hypotheses to the Iranian and Nicaraguan cases. This is why I have reformulated some parts of her argument while rejecting others. These modifications bring forth the question of why I continue to insist on the usefulness of her approach. In other words, given the extent to which I have altered the specifics of her argument, why should *States and Social Revolutions* still be considered an important learning source for the study of contemporary revolutions? The answer to this question can be found in Skocpol's version of the structural approach; that is, in her argument that once we grasp the dynamics of social structure—their "logic"—we can also begin to understand change, since knowledge of structure gives us clues about what is possible, what shapes the possibilities, and what defines the limits of human action.[7] Skocpol's work is especially useful because she has articulated differences and similarities in the structures and conjunctures of the prerevolutionary and postrevolutionary societies she compares. Furthermore, by connecting these structures and conjunctures to the larger world-historical context, she has elucidated the problems, limits, and choices forced on actors in periods of revolutionary crisis.

As Skocpol herself points out, these problems, limits, and choices forced on actors change from case to case. They were even different in the revolutionary cases she studied. She has nevertheless been able to lay out certain generalizations from which we can learn. We can learn from them because they direct our attention to certain relationships, possibilities, and conjunctures that may be conducive to social change in a revolutionary form. But, for two reasons, these generalizations are not—and Skocpol knows this—"cause," in the sense of high-level generalizations explaining law-like and historically invariant connections. First, learning about social structures of a society in crisis the way Skocpol proposes does not mean that the specific and very different conditions making up the events can be ignored. Second, any explanatory scheme within a changing world-historical context needs to take into account those relatively enduring, but also changing, structures that condition, limit, and enable actors whose particular actions constitute human history. It is my hope that the preceding chapters not only have brought out the historical specifities of the Iranian and Nicaraguan revolutions but also have shed light on the changing social structures in the larger world-historical context.

NOTES

1. The format of this synopsis is based on the questions posed in the introduction.

2. My understanding of politics in the Philippines has been influenced by papers presented at the Conference on Local Perspectives on Political Change in the Philippines, at the University of Hawaii at Manoa, May 16–18, 1988.

3. See W. L. Goldfrank, "World System, State Structure, and the Onset of the Mexican Revolution," *Politics and Society* 5, 4 (1979), pp. 97–134, and W. L. Goldfrank, "Theories of Revolution and Revolution without Theory: The Case of Mexico," *Theory and Society* 7 (January–March 1979), pp. 97–134.

4. On Cuba, see J. O'Connor, *The Origins of Cuban Socialism* (Ithaca, N.Y.: Cornell University Press, 1970).

5. R. Armstrong, "El Salvador: Why Revolution," in *Revolution in Central America*, ed. The Stanford Central American Action Network (Boulder, Colo.: Westview Press, 1983).

6. R. Armstrong and J. Shenk, "El Salvador, a Revolution Brews," in ibid.

7. This interpretation of Skcopol's structural approach, and much of the argument that follows, is influenced by the numerous conversations I have had with Peter Manicas.

Index

Jahad-e Sazandegi (Crusade for
Constructiveness), 119
Japan: economic development in, 36; revolu-
tion from above in, 8
Judiciary reform, in Iran, 107, 108, 125*n*
July 26 movement in Cuba, 97
Jung, Harold, 41, 61*n*

Kaimowitz, David, 123*n*, 126*n*, 129*n*
Katouzian, H., 61*n*, 79*n*, 80*n*
Kazemi, Farhad, 25*n*, 70, 71, 79*n*, 80*n*
Kazemzadeh, F., 57*n*
Keddie, N. R., 57*n*, 63*n*, 79*n*, 87–88, 95,
102*n*, 103*n*, 104*n*
Kennedy, John, 48
Khadim, M., 128*n*
Khamenei, Mohammad Ali, 128*n*
Khomeini, Ayatollah Ruhollah, 52, 120,
127*n*; abortive uprising led by, 94; exile
of, 57*n*; and Islamic Nationalism, 92–93;
rise of, 92–93; support of, for Bani Sadr,
127*n*; suspension of IRP activities by, 120
Khuzistan, 69

Labor force: in Iran, 21*n*, 69; in Nicaragua,
21*n*, 73, 129*n*
Ladjevardi, H., 57*n*
Lake, A., 63*n*
Lambton, A. K. S., 57
Lancaster, R. N., 104–5*n*
Land ownership, in Iran, 56–57*n*
Land reform, in Nicaragua, 40; in pre-
revolutionary Iran, 68–69; in post-
revolutionary Iran, 107–8. *See also*
Agrarian reform
Latin American Bishops' Conference in
Medellín, Colombia, 75, 99
LeoGrande, William, 48, 49, 61*n*, 63*n*
León, 30, 73
Leonese (Nicaragua), 30, 58*n*
Levi, M., 23*n*
Levine, D. H., 104*n*
Liberalization, 51
Liberation theology, in Nicaragua, 6, 104–5*n*
Literacy rate: in Iran, 21*n*; in Nicaragua, 21*n*
Luciak, I. A., 126*n*, 129*n*

McDonough, P., 23*nn*
Managua, 73; 1972 earthquake, 41, 74, 75.
See also Nicaragua

Manicas, Peter, 138*n*
Marchetti, P., 126*n*
Marcos, Ferdinand, downfall of, 133
Marginal bourgeoisie, in Nicaragua, 41
Martí, José, 97
Marx, Karl, 15, 22*n*
Marxian analysis, 15–16, 23*n*; and theory
of change, 15
Marxism, 24*n*
Marxist-Christian dialogue, in Nicaragua,
96–100, 112, 121
Masaya, 73
Mashhad, 80*n*
Massing, M., 129*n*
Mass military mobilization, in Nicaragua,
112, 127*n*
Medellín conference. *See* Latin American
Bishops' Conference
Mexican Revolution, 132, 133. *See also*
Díaz, Porfirio
Mexico: political crisis in, 134; U.S.
involvement in, 46, 133
Military: in Iran, 33; in Nicaragua, 33,
54–55, 107. *See also* National
Guard
Ministry of Revolutionary Guards, in Iran,
125*n*
Mojahedin-e Khalq, 72, 93, 116, 127*n*
Monimbo: description of, 74–75; insurrec-
tion in, 67
Moore, B., Jr., 20*n*
Morley, Morris, 35, 59*n*
Mossadeq, Mohammad: ouster of, 28–29,
134; as prime minister, 28; relationship
with the left, 29; support for, 29, 134,
135; U.S. backed military coup to
remove, 29, 57*n*
Mottaheri, Morteza, 104*n*
MPU. *See* United People's Movement

Nairn, Tom, 24*n*
National Front: creation of, in Iran, 28; effort
of in mobilization of urban poor, 70–71,
134. *See also* Farabundo Martí National
Liberation Front (FMLN); Sandinista
National Liberation Front (FSLN)
National Guard, in Nicaragua, 31, 33–34,
53–55, 64*n*, 76
National Iranian Oil Company (NIOC), 57*n*
Nationalism, 24*n*; and capitalism, 36; as

Note on the Author

Farideh Farhi received her Ph.D. in political science from the University of Colorado at Boulder in 1986. She currently teaches comparative politics at the University of Hawaii at Manoa.